PUBLICATIONS OF THE TEXAS FOLKLORE SOCIETY

NUMBER XXIV

MODY C. BOATRIGHT, *Editor*

The Healer of Los Olmos
and Other Mexican Lore

PUBLISHED BY SOUTHERN METHODIST UNIVERSITY PRESS

The Healer of Los Olmos
and Other Mexican Lore

Edited by

Wilson M. Hudson

Southern Methodist University Press

Dallas

HOW THIS BOOK TOOK SHAPE

WHEN MR. Mody C. Boatright, General Editor for the Texas Folklore Society, left for California to teach in the early part of the summer, he entrusted me with the editorship of our annual publication for 1951. He suggested that we limit contributions to Mexican materials.

Before leaving, Mr. Boatright turned over to me a study made by Miss Soledad Pérez under his direction. Fortunately Miss Pérez had planned to attend The University of Texas in the summer. With my advice she has prepared her manuscript for publication.

Mr. J. Frank Dobie was the means of my obtaining Miss Ruth Dodson's contribution. When I expressed an interest in Mexican folk medicine, he lent me her Spanish book on Don Pedrito Jaramillo. Translations of parts of this, I thought, would give value to our publication. In her reply to my inquiry, Miss Dodson informed me that she had already translated her book and made some additions to it besides. She sent me the manuscript and I decided to include most of her stories about the healer of Los Olmos.

Since our publication was to consist of Mexican lore, I prevailed upon Mr. Dobie, who has told many Mexican tales for English readers, to make a contribution. He had just finished his manuscript on the mustang, but I gave him no rest until I had his essay in my hands.

My own two stories, collected some time ago in Jalisco, seemed to fit in with the other contributions.

Mr. José Cisneros of El Paso was kind enough to draw the illustrations for our book.

WILSON M. HUDSON
Austin, Texas
1 September 1951

TABLE OF CONTENTS

Page

CHARM IN MEXICAN FOLKTALES—*J. Frank Dobie* 1
DON PEDRITO JARAMILLO: THE CURANDERO OF LOS
    OLMOS—*Ruth Dodson* 9
Why This Was Written 9
The Life of Don Pedrito Jaramillo: Benefactor of
    Humanity 11
Dionisio Tells of His Cures 18
An Early Memory of Don Pedrito 20
Don Juan and Don Pedrito 20
How Señora Tomasita de Canales Was Cured 22
Tomás Flores Had No Regrets 24
The Bewitched Woman 25
An Ax in the Hand and Faith in the Heart 27
Mabel Sutherland Remembers Don Pedrito 28
Borrowed Shoes 31
Chat Vela and the Brujo 31
When One Brings a Lie 32
Cured with a Lemon 33
Without Looking Back 34
Baths and Beer 35
A Sure Cure for Migraine Headache 36
The Growth That Vanished 36
An Epileptic Is Cured 37
Cure of a Horsebreaker 38
Various Cures 39
A Grassburr in His Throat 40
A Citizen of León, Mexico, Visits Texas 40
The Namesake in New Mexico 41
The Night of the New Moon 42
From the North 42
Without the Doctor's Knowledge 43
A Hot Bath for Fever 44
Half a Glass of Tepid Water 45
Nosebleed 45
Three Leaves of Prickly Pear 45
Escape from a Mad Dog 46
The Cure of a Horse 46
Mysterious Money 47
The Marvelous Cure of a Shepherd 49

Cured of Drinking 49
Don Pedrito Sings 50
At Midnight in a Lake 50
Bowlegs 51
The Cripple 51
Diego Was Cured 52
The Spade and the Hoe 52
To Be Well in March 53
God Cured Him 54
Asthma for Life 54
Complete But for One Son 55
Not a Turkey Egg 55
A Vaquero Who Failed to Follow Directions .. 56
Faith Healed Him 56
Soldier Herb 57
Susto Cured by Susto 57
Nine Onions and Nine Baths 58
Little Petra 59
The Church Bell 60
From the Town of Refugio 62
The Vow Fulfilled 62
The Spirit of Don Pedrito Gives Hope 63
Señora María Saenz 65
Don Pedrito's Spirit in Monterrey 65
The Stranger at the Grave 66
Copies of Written Prescriptions 67
A Backward Glance 68
MEXICAN FOLKLORE FROM AUSTIN, TEXAS—*Soledad Pérez* 71
Conditions of Collection 71
The Weeping Woman 73
The Return of the Gardener 77
The Fat Man 78
The Wandering Prince 80
Ratoncito Pérez 81
The Real 84
Tales of the Devil 86
    The Stranger 86
    Lidia and the Devil 86
    Matasiete 87
    The Ball of Fire 88
    The Spotted Pooch 89
    The Sow in the Plaza 90

Ghost Tales 90
  The Cold, Clammy Hand.................... 90
  La Esperanza 91
  A Visit with the Dead..................... 92
  The Midnight Call......................... 93
  Indian Rendezvous 94
  A Dead Man Speaks........................ 94
  The German Girl.......................... 95
Tales of Buried Treasure...................... 96
  Treasure at the Hacienda de los Albarcones...... 96
  Horses' Hoofbeats 99
  The Smugglers' Treasure................... 99
  A Strange Animal......................... 100
  A White Light............................ 100
  The Stagecoach 101
Saints' Miracles 102
  Innocence Proved 102
  The Saint Who Disappeared................ 102
  "El Niño Perdido"........................ 103
  The Protection of the Saints.............. 103
  St. Anthony Performs a Miracle............ 104
  The Virgin 104
  The Traveler 105
  Benito Cásarez 106
Remedies 106
Beliefs and Superstitions..................... 114
Proverbs and Sayings......................... 118
Riddles 126
To Whom God Wishes to Give He Will Give—
  Wilson M. Hudson........................ 128
The Fisherman and the Snake of Many Colors—
  Wilson M. Hudson........................ 132
Illustrations—José Cisneros
  The Marvelous Cure of a Shepherd......... 48
  The Weeping Woman...................... 75
  Ratoncito Pérez 82
  The Fisherman and the Snake of Many Colors...... 133
Index 137

J. FRANK DOBIE, *a mainstay of the Texas Folklore Society for many years, has done more than anyone else to bring to light the literary resources of the Southwest. As a teacher, editor, and author he has led the way, encouraging others as well as writing in an engaging and thorough fashion about almost every phase of Southwestern life. To his great books on the longhorn and the coyote, he will soon add another on the mustang.*

CHARM IN MEXICAN FOLKTALES

By J. FRANK DOBIE

A GREAT DEAL of folklore is inane, banal, stupid, dull, and tedious. Nobody should feel under compulsion to "preserve it for posterity." Indeed, the only possible way for posterity to survive is to ignore most of what our posterity-conscious age is hoarding for it. That is exactly what posterity will do. Think of all the tinhorn newspapers sealed up in corner-stones for posterity, of all the glowworm lucubrations in the ever-enlarging local historical quarterlies, of all the army deadbeats commissioned to write regimental histories, and of all the acres of fireproof vaults built to hold them!

Next to catalogues of superstitions, perhaps the most deadening form of folklore is the tall tale that has no other quality than tallness. It has come to be as American as con-gressional committees to preserve Americanism. As cheap money drives out sound money, it is running the genuine folktale out of circulation. Any adding machine can make one. These tall tales that have no other quality than tallness are as devoid of imaginative qualities, of humanity and charm, as jokes manufactured for the radio and Bennett Cerf's books. They take their flavor from sawdust and the mass production line. They are never childlike in natural-ness and simplicity; they are invariably puerile. I am not talking about tall tales validated by wit and ingenuity, though the best of these rate low unless they are seasoned with the salt of humanity.

There are only three forms of folklore that people really

enjoy. They are songs, tales, and pithy sayings. The remainder belongs to social history. The best American folktales that I know date from preradio times. Yet age alone tells nothing about, adds nothing to, quality. Nearly all the tales on David Crockett were manufactured by almanac makers, and, as Richard Dorson has abundantly shown—though he intended to show something else,—they are tedious beyond words. Bigfoot Wallace's yarns of the same period, full of exaggeration, are delectable. Bigfoot Wallace did not have the mental cast of the manufacturer of almanac and radio jokes. He was of the earth earthy; as Goethe said of Englishmen, he had the courage—though I think he was unconscious of it—to be what nature had made him. Of course he was not a writer. The few of his yarns we know have come through other men.

Charm is a rare quality in all forms of literature. A majority of the folktales of the Southwest that have charm are Mexican. Those that are not Mexican but that set the imagination a-traveling often have a kind of Mexican touch. This is especially true of tales about buried treasure and lost mines.

I know of only two Billy the Kid stories that have charm. One, a narrative of an episode in which the writer took part, is by R. B. Townshend, a cultivated Englishman, in *The Tenderfoot in New Mexico*. The other is a folktale, "Interim," truly delicious, in Frank Applegate's *Native Tales of New Mexico*. American tales about bad men of the Southwest, those written by journalists in particular, generally have about as much charm as a hogshead of stale blood. Perhaps Jim Bowie is not to be classed as a bad man. His knife was a personal thing, not something off the assembly line, and some of the tales about his use of it belong in the tradition of Norse tales about great swords and swordsmen.

In the realm of true stories, some of which become traditional in all lands and thus pass into folklore, Anglo-American tellings are richer, go deeper into life, and are better told than Mexican. I can illustrate from a collection of tales on one subject that I spent years in gathering from men of the range, both Mexican and American, and also from printed sources. I refer to the combination of history and narrative in my book *The Longhorns*. Most of the stories could be classified as realistic. Of three that I think of as having charm, two are folkloric in nature and came from Mexican vaqueros. The other—the story of tamale-eating, home-returning Sancho—came from a Celt. All three tellers, to quote Matthew Arnold's words, lived "in reaction against the despotism of fact." All three outvisualized any camera. But it is quality in detail, and not mere detail, that gives charm.

I will retell one of these tales because it illustrates characteristics I am trying to define: charm, a certain unworldly flavor, a peculiar kind of lightsomeness, even though attached to something as heavy as a bull, a passing beyond the walls of the prison house that close us in. It was told to me by an old, spent vaquero named José Beltrán one winter afternoon beside a fire of mesquite wood burning in a fireplace on the Tom O'Connor ranch near Refugio, Texas. We had been talking about wild cattle, some of them outlaw steers, some of them mavericks, roped in the brush and trapped in pens at watering places. Nobody was around to cramp José Beltrán's style. He was little, lithe, black, and bowlegged, with eyes that gleamed and peered everywhere. In telling a story he could not sit still. He stood, knelt, bent over on all fours, squatted, jumped up, looked out yonder, seeing whatever he was talking about. He imitated the sound of hoofbeats, the bark of a coyote, the bleat of a calf, the mumbling of a bull, the scuttling of an armadillo. He talked with his hands as much as with his mouth. I found myself jumping up and sitting down, looking and listening with him.

He began trapping wild cattle on the O'Connor ranch not long after windmills were built there. One mill was over a well at the Mexican Water Hole. It and a dirt tank and troughs were enclosed by a big pen made of slick wire doubled around high posts set deep in the ground. No animal could jump the fence or knock it down. At one corner a gate opened into a small holding pen, equally strong. The gate from the pasture into the big watering pen was wide, and it was always left open so that cattle could enter at will, the wildest ones becoming used to it. A light wire led from the gate to the windmill platform, about thirty-five feet high. When it was time to trap wild cattle, the trapper sat on the platform and watched and waited until animals he wanted to catch came inside; then he shut the gate by pulling the wire.

Bueno, José Beltrán said, when Don Patricio Lambert told me to go to the Mexican Water Hole, he sent another vaquero with me. We hide our horses way off, way off, out of the wind. We do not walk through the gate and leave our smell. No, we climb over wire at a place where the cattle do not come.

It is hot summer. We take off our clothes and bury them in sand. The body of a man, just in his own skin, does not give out scent like the clothes he has sweat in. We rub dirt and cow manure all over our bodies and in our hair. Now we do not stink like a man at all. We go to the windmill tower. There is a bucket. I take water in it out of the trough and pour water on our tracks. We touch nothing. Then we climb up.

On top we take off our shoes, so a step on the planks will not make one sound. We sit down. I face the gate, and the other vaquero is watching too. The wire is ready to pull. The moon is bright like day. We wait and wait. There is nothing. I see a coyote that wants some water. He makes no sound. We wait and wait. I hear maybeso one armadillo in the sticks, outside the pen. One hour, two hours, three hours pass. Now I think nothing is coming tonight. Wild cattle do not come in after midnight, until about five o'clock in the morning.

My *compañero* and I do not speak all this time, except with a finger and *ssh,* like that. I am nearly asleep. Then I hear from the trail in the brush one bull. *Bru-uh-uh,* he says, not loud, low down in himself. *Shh.*

Good, I think. He is bringing some cattle with him. In the summer the bulls do not stay by themselves as in the cold time. He makes that talk again, *Bru-uh-uh,* low, quiet, like the night. He is closer. Then in that bright moonlight I see him at the gate. He is black, black, *puro negro.* He stops and smells the ground and the posts. I am looking for the other cattle. He stands a long time, listening, looking.

Then, after long time, he comes in, all alone. He walks straight to the trough. I can hear him drinking, *hillkk, hillkk*. He drinks until he is full. He stands one little minute with his head towards the gate. He belches—that way. I am looking for the other cattle. Still they do not come. I can see the unmarked ears on the black bull. Now he starts for the gate.

I pull the wire. I hear the gate slam. Then I hear *psh-hh-hh*. I tell this vaquero to go open the gate to the little pen in the corner and when I scare the bull through it, to shut it. I go easy to the fence, in the direction away from the bull, and climb over and go around on the outside to the big gate in front of the bull. I will scare the bull and make him run to the corner and go into the little pen. He will fight with me if I am inside with him. But outside I can play with him.

But the bull is not at the gate. I look and look. I go all around the pen, looking through the wire, looking in the bright moonlight. There is no brush in the pen, just one huisache and six, eight mesquites. The other vaquero he looks too. There is no black bull in the pen. No, do not deceive yourself into thinking any bull could jump that fence, that gate.

Listen. This bull is not one bull. He is *el diablo*. I do not wish to stay at the Mexican Water Hole longer that night. Maybeso it is the Devil's Water Hole. We put on our clothes and ride to the ranch. Nobody ever saw that maverick bull again. Nobody ever saw him before that night. What does this seem to you?

I have not said or meant to imply that the interesting folktales of the Southwest are all Mexican. However, the only really interesting tale about a burro, a very common and representative subject, that I know of is Mexican; this tale is also delectable, charming. Under title of "Old Juan Mora's Burro," it is in the book by Frank Applegate already cited. No American sophisticated in the common way ever refers to a burro except in a patronizing manner. No charm nor any other good quality ever comes out of patronization

—and patronization is what untempered mechanical superiority brings.

Take the subject of coyotes. I claim to have read and heard as many stories on coyotes as anybody alive. I put many, the best I could find, in a book. From some points of view the most interesting are from individuals who studied the coyote as an animal; they are realistic. The most unrealistic are Indian tales of mythological import, and generally they seem stupid to civilized minds. Indianized Spaniards, or Spanishized Indians, the *mestizo* Mexicans, subtracted the mythological from coyote tales, added the ironic and something else, and generated a cycle of tales often ridiculously unrealistic and just as often delightful in a play-world way. Irony goes well with charm—and where can one find the blend more lightsomely and more intricately made than in J. M. Barrie?—in *Rosalind,* for example. I would say that the Spaniard is too dry and ironic for the blend and the Indian too respectful of his own heritage. The *mestizo* makes it better. A little tale I heard in New Mexico illustrates it.

One time a burro driver was beating the whey out of his son Francisco when a friend appeared.

"But, compadre," the friend exclaimed, "why are you thus without mercy lashing our Francisco?"

"I'll tell you," replied the burro driver. "Here I have been making plans for the time when I am rich. I will have a cow. She will give so much milk that we will have all we can drink and all the cheese we can eat. Besides that, we will have cheese to sell. We will have money to throw at the birds. One thing I will buy will be a blue bowl. It will be a beautiful bowl, as blue as the sky, with little painted figures on it coming up to the rim so that they can look over inside at the beautiful white milk.

"And here, compadre, I have been telling my sons how the beautiful blue bowl full of milk will be set on the board with Francisco on one side of it and Juanito on the other side of it. Francisco can drink out of his side of the blue bowl and Juanito can drink out of his side. But listen! This burro of a Francisco says he will not drink out of the blue bowl with his brother. Now, compadre, you comprehend with what reason I beat him."

One could read through hundreds of Mexican tales published in the *Journal of American Folklore* without finding more than a modicum of charm. The listener who would bring it out from a teller must have it inside himself. They fertilize each other. Somehow it eludes recording machines, whether of flesh or metal. Probably no printed folktale that can be called an example of finished art is a literal transcription of an oral telling. Art is as long in a folktale as in any other form.

Charm does not belong, of course, to any nationality. Yet one finds it in W. H. Hudson's tales and recollections of the pampas, where he listened to the gauchos and the curlews, as nowhere else in his writings. One would not find it in talk of an Argentine or Mexican Rotary Club any more than in the talk of a Chicago Rotary Club. An extensive class of Mexican tales is devoid of it—tales designed to cultivate credulity in fatuous miracles. Charm goes with skepticism more often than with credulity.

Charm comes out of the earth and also out of the highest form of sophistication. Yet no amount of sophistication can produce it. It is innate, like dignity and winsomeness. The only point I started out to make, however, is that charm as a distinguishing quality in folktales of the Southwest belongs peculiarly to Mexican tales. One final illustration is borrowed from *Tongues of the Monte*—a book in which I tried to weave a pattern of Mexican folklife and folklore. This tale, like many tales that employ irony, makes a point on human conduct, but somehow avoids didacticism, which is nearly always pedestrian.

One time, Inocencio began, a hunter who had never been able to kill a deer, although he had hunted often in good deer country, came upon a big buck asleep. This buck was standing under a spreading tree and the hunter was looking over a boulder so close to him that he could see the hairs on his side move under the breathing. As the hunter looked at the big buck there so near and so still, he was very happy. At last he was sure of game. And as he leveled his gun, very slowly, to fire, his head filled with plans.

"I'll take all that meat home to my family," he said to

himself, "and I'll cure the hide and make moccasins out of it. I'll wear one pair of the *teguas,* and I'll trade two pairs off for a calf. The calf will grow to be a cow and she will have other calves. While we are having plenty of cheese, one of these calves will grow to be a fine, strong ox. I'll trade him off for a mare. The mare will have a colt, and I'll trade him off for a jack. Then the jack and the mare will bring mules. I'll just raise mules—mules—mules. There'll be one mule at first, then two mules, then three mules, then four, then five, then six, seven, eight. I shall not be driving another man's mules any longer at peon wages. I'll be carrying freight by contract!"

The string of mules filed by in front of the hunter's eyes so that he could not see the big buck asleep. He saw them all loaded with *cargas* and he saw himself as the *conductor* of a whole *recua* of pack mules, a hired *arriero* helping him. He saw the mules stringing out along the trail to Chihuahua. He could keep himself silent no longer. At the top of his voice he yelled, *"Hi-lo!"* ("String out!"—the cry of mule driver and vaquero.)

The big buck awoke with a jump and was out of shot in the brush before the hunter could aim. As it is said, the Indian, the bird, and the deer are gone when they are gone. He who with his arms engirdles much can squeeze little.

Ruth Dodson *belongs to one of the oldest ranching families in South Texas. She was born and reared on a ranch in Nueces County some twenty-five miles north of Alice. She knows the Mexicans of that part of Texas "better than they know themselves," to quote Mr. J. Frank Dobie. She lives in Alice at the present time.*

Don Pedrito Jaramillo

THE CURANDERO OF LOS OLMOS

WHY THIS WAS WRITTEN

The first time I ever heard of Pedro Jaramillo, the Mexican faith healer sometimes called the Benefactor of Humanity and known among the Mexican people as Don Pedrito, was in the early nineties, in 1893 to be exact. It was a time of great drought in South Texas, as it is now in the year 1950. My father and oldest brother had gone to hunt pasturage for our starving cattle. In their search they went south, into what was known as the Sands, a strip of country lying along what now is the highly developed valley of the Rio Grande.

After traveling something like sixty miles from Lost Ranch, our home, a two days' journey on horseback, they passed near the well-known Mexican ranch headquarters of Los Olmos (The Elms), where Don Pedro Jaramillo had come to make his home and practice his calling. Rancho Los Olmos was located not far north of present-day Falfurrias, which was settled after the railroad was extended from Alice in 1903.

As my father and brother rode along through the thinly populated, drought-stricken, sandy country, finding it in no better condition than the part of the country they had left, they came to a lake now almost dry. In the middle of it, they said, wallowing around in the muddy water was a nude Mexican man. They thought that he was surely a demented person who had wandered away from his home and was not responsible for what he was doing. They stopped and called to him for an explanation. He told them that he was following a prescription given him by Don Pedrito Jaramillo, the faith healer at Los Olmos Ranch.

What the man's ailment was or how successful the treatment proved, we had no way of knowing. But this incident served to acquaint us with the faith healer and something of his methods.

Before long we began hearing more of this unique curandero, especially through the Mexican people of the locality in which we lived. And from that time until his death in 1907, we were familiar with the stories that were being told of Don Pedrito and his work as a faith healer.

Then one hot summer day, an old Mexican man I had known all my life came to my house to tell me that Don Pedrito had died. He told me the news in the manner of closing a story, which was the way I accepted it: *"Ya murió Don Pedrito,"* Trinidad announced to me as he came in— "Now Don Pedrito has died." He seemed to imply that there was nothing more to be said for him, that his career was finished.

Twenty-five years passed. Then when I was writing something on folk curing among the Mexicans for the Texas Folklore Society, I recalled the Mexican curandero, the faith healer of Los Olmos. He had occupied a superior place among folk healers. I thought something of his work should be set down in writing. I asked Mr. J. Frank Dobie, who was for many years editor of the Texas Folklore Society publications, if anyone else had done so. He replied that no one had. So I included Don Pedrito in my "Folk-Curing Among the Mexicans."[1]

I investigated to see if any of the Mexicans I came in contact with could tell me anything about Don Pedrito and his work. I found that stories about his cures had become a well-established tradition among the Mexican population. I found that many who had known him and had gone to him for help while he lived were taking their medicines and

[1]In *Tone the Bell Easy,* Texas Folklore Society Publication X (1932), 82-98.

teaching their descendants to take their medicines "In the name of God, and in the name of Don Pedrito."

Then I decided to collect and write down the stories the people told about this man and have them made into a little book. Since most of these stories would be told to me by Spanish-speaking people, I decided to write the book in Spanish. It appeared in 1934 under the imprint of Casa Editorial Lozana, at San Antonio, Texas.

Almost at once after it was published, I received a request from the Library of the College of Physicians in Philadelphia, the oldest medical school in the United States, for donation of a copy. I was glad to forward one and thus place a record of Don Pedro Jaramillo in a position of note and permanency, even though the record was in Spanish. Now my wish is to present the same record in English. I have added several stories not among those in the Spanish book, and I have brought the account down to the year 1950.

THE LIFE OF DON PEDRO JARAMILLO
BENEFACTOR OF HUMANITY

"HERE LIE the remains of Pedro Jaramillo the Benefactor of Humanity. Born in Guadalajara, Jalisco, Mexico. Died at Paisano, Starr County, Texas, July 3, 1907."

This is the epitaph, written in Spanish, on a small stone in the form of a cross that marks the grave of an old Mexican faith healer in a small cemetery near Falfurrias in South Texas, in what now is Brooks County.

Pedro Jaramillo came to this part of Texas from Mexico in 1881. His interest in the locality developed through a friend in Mexico who knew this country. He first came in the company of some men who were bringing liquors to Las Cabras Ranch of Don Andrés Canales, where a celebration was to be held on St. John's Day, June 24, which festival was widely celebrated on Mexican ranches in those days. This gave Don Pedro an opportunity to see something of the country.

He went back to Mexico and then returned to settle at Los Olmos Ranch. This was another of the large Mexican ranches that were situated in the then thinly populated part of Texas between the Nueces River and the Rio Grande. He announced himself as a *curandero,* a healer, and settled at Los Olmos Ranch in the neighborhood of present-day Falfurrias. At that time there was only one doctor between Corpus Christi and Laredo, at San Diego, and the Mexicans would have preferred to consult a curandero even if doctors had been plentiful.

He claimed that God had bestowed on him the power to heal the sick; to say which prescription, given in the name of God and executed with faith and in the name of God, had power to heal. He claimed no healing power of himself. His mission was to help the sick through their faith in God's power to heal them.

He made no charges for the prescriptions; the patients gave whatever they cared to, or nothing at all; nevertheless, what the people gave voluntarily was sufficient for Don Pedro, who himself often gave to the poor and the sick who came to him. For himself he wanted only enough for his very frugal living. He thought that since God had bestowed on him the power to help humanity, he could also take that power away from him if he used it for his own benefit.

The story of how this gift of healing was bestowed on Pedro Jaramillo was told to me something like thirty years ago by a man who lived at Los Olmos and who said that he had been born and reared there. He said that he, when a boy, heard "Don Pedrito," as he became known to everyone, tell it to his father.

Don Pedrito related that when he was a poor laborer in Mexico (some say he was a shepherd), working for half a bushel of corn and the equivalent of five dollars a month, he suffered an affliction of the nose (his picture shows a prominent scar just below the bridge). One night, he said, he was suffering so much that he went out into the woods to a pool of water. He lay down and buried his face in the mud at the edge. This relieved him. He stayed here treating himself with the mud. At the end of three days he was well; but his nose remained disfigured. (This disfiguration of the nose is always associated with the gift of healing that is credited to Don Pedrito.)

He returned to his house and lay down and slept. After a while a voice awakened him and told him that he had received from God the gift of healing. At the same time, the voice told him that his master was sick and that he had the power to cure him. He got up and went to his master. He prescribed the first thing that came into his mind. After this manner he prescribed always. In this case the prescription was a tepid bath daily for three days. His master followed this prescription and recovered. Thus began the work of this curandero.

At his new home, on Los Olmos Creek, his work began among the families at Los Olmos Ranch and the neighboring ranches. It grew to a marvelous extent until it finally covered hundreds of square miles. It lasted a full twenty-five years.

During the first years, it was very difficult to contact a great many of the people. Only through long hard trips could it be done. At this time Don Pedrito made trips on horseback far from his home, sometimes accompanied by an old man, a friend. He would go to Corpus Christi, San Antonio, and Laredo. He would stop at intermediate points, and in this manner he saw thousands of people who were sick and wanted his help.

On one of these trips to San Antonio, it is said, the crowd became so great that the police were called out. The doctors took notice and made an investigation to see by what authority Don Pedrito practiced. They found that they could do nothing to restrain him because he made no charges for his prescriptions.

When Don Pedrito went away on a trip, he left at home groceries to feed the people who came from a distance and waited for his return. These groceries were brought by wagon and team from the town of Alice, forty miles away. When his work was well established, a grocery merchant said, he would buy four or five hundred dollars' worth of groceries at a time. This merchant also said that Don Pedrito was the only customer he had who bought an entire barrel of cube sugar in one order. He would sometimes prescribe the sugar and furnish the patient with the remedy.

He kept the groceries in a lumber room built for that purpose and called "the store," but nothing was sold; where need existed, food was given.

One of his friends, Don Antonio Hinojosas, made him a present of a hundred acres of land. This he developed into a farm. He fenced it, put a small house and a well on it, and set someone to work it. Here he raised corn for the making of tortillas (the daily bread of the Mexican in those days), watermelons, cashaws (the long-necked pumpkin that the Mexican prefers to other varieties), peppers, garbanzos (chick-peas), and garlic. Whatever came off the farm went into Don Pedrito's work. What the curandero received with one hand he gave away with the other.

When Don Pedrito had been at Los Olmos about ten years a most terrible drought visited the country. It began in 1893 and lasted several years. "There was dearth in the land," as the Bible poetically says; but the plain meaning is want, scarcity, and famine. Don Albino Canales, son of Don Andrés Canales of Las Cabras Ranch, who was a small boy at the time, says that Don Pedrito practically fed the northern part of Starr County (now part of Brooks County). Then the State sent some help in the form of corn and beans. And Don Pedrito was selected among those to distribute the food.

Don Pedrito employed people to do the work about his place and to look after and help those who came.

John Sutherland, whose father was postmaster at Los Olmos for a number of years, told me that at times there would be as many as five hundred people camped on Los Olmos Creek awaiting the return of Don Pedrito. Some came for miles on foot, others on horseback, others in wagons and buggies. An entire family might come bringing one sick member, and at the same time a man might arrive horseback to ask for remedies for several of his family, his relatives and friends; and it could have been that this man had traveled a hundred miles or more to see Don Pedrito.

When Don Pedrito was at home, he would go into his *jacal*, or hut, and sit down behind a table. A man he employed directed the people who passed before him. They told the nature of their sickness or not, it is said, for Don Pedrito knew without being told. (He is credited with having had clairvoyant as well as mind-reading power.) When he gave the prescription—sometimes orally, sometimes written down—the patient would place what he cared to give on the table. To some patients the curandero would say, "No, keep your money; you need it for your trip home." Or again he would say, "No, return it to whom you borrowed it from." In this way he dispatched the people easily and quickly.

After Don Pedrito had lived at Los Olmos for some time, a post office was established there with the name of Paisano. The mail was first brought by a mailcarrier on horseback; later it came by stagecoach on the run from Alice to Brownsville. Then much of Don Pedrito's work was done by mail. In the many letters he received, sometimes as many as two hundred a week, were enclosed stamps or money. Of the stamps there were enough for the replies, and finally enough to fill a large box.

The register of the post office showed that many letters were sent out but that the stamps sold were not equal in number to the letters mailed. For this reason an investigation was made from the Post Office Department in Washington. The investigator was not convinced until he saw the amount of stamps that Don Pedrito had collected at his house.

When the railroad reached the new town of Falfurrias in 1903, something like twenty years after Don Pedrito had come to Los Olmos and only four years before his death, then many sick people came on the train. A man at Los Olmos established the business of transporting the people back and forth the four miles between the railroad station at Falfurrias and Don Pedrito's home at Los Olmos. This man had four vehicles that at times made three or four trips a day, bringing the people to get prescriptions, and taking those away who had been prescribed for.

The work of this curandero was not confined to his own people. He prescribed for many of the Americans. And all those who knew him and his work were convinced that he was a good man, charitable and sincere; one who believed that he had a God-given mission to perform and dedicated all his time, efforts, and money to that end.

Nevertheless, his work caused him to meet with disapproval by some doctors and officers of the places he visited. It is said that he was suspected in Mexico and at one time put in jail there, but the charge against him of being a *brujo* (wizard) was not strong enough to justify his being held. The late Dr. J. S. Strickland, who knew Don Pedrito better than any other doctor in the country, who covered the same territory he did, and who no doubt treated the same patients at times when neither knew it, said that Don Pedrito was a smart but uneducated man, and that he did perform wonderful cures. Mrs. N. A. Hoffman of San Diego tells that she heard Dr. Strickland say, when someone suggested to him that the curandero be prohibited from doing his work, "No, how do I know that Don Pedrito's prayers don't do more good than my pills?"

And there was the saintly parish priest, Father Bard, located some fifty miles from Don Pedrito, who was within the priest's parish. When one of his altar boys, Lafayette Wright, was inclined to make light of Don Pedrito and his remedies, Father Bard reproved him. He explained that God, knowing of the great need of the people where there were so few doctors, saw fit to bestow on this humble man the power of helping these people. He had endowed him for the work. And the servant fulfilled his vocation faithfully.

It can be said that there has never been another so honored and appreciated among the Mexican people of South Texas as this curandero, this folk healer, Pedro Jaramillo. It can also be said that no one else in this part of the country, of whatever nationality, religion, economic or social standing, has done, through a lifetime, as much to try to relieve human suffering as this man did through the twenty-five years that he lived in South Texas. He gave to his work the days of his life and the many thousands of dollars presented by those who felt that they had been helped through him.

And now, forty-odd years after his death, the Mexican

people are holding this folk character, this "Benefactor of Humanity," in still greater reverence as time passes. They regard him as a saint, which attitude he discouraged during his lifetime. He told his patients repeatedly, "I have no healing power. It is the power of God released through your faith which heals you."

Today, pictures of Don Pedrito are placed among those of the saints in the homes of Mexicans of South Texas, and small statues copied from his picture are kept in their homes too. Masses are often said for the repose of his soul in the churches of the region where many people still remember him. And in many homes a place of honor is given to an enlarged picture of the curandero. A firm in Laredo that supplies curative herbs uses his picture and the trademark, "Don Pedrito."

On last All Souls' Day, in 1950, seventy years after he first came to Los Olmos Ranch—now a ghost ranch itself—people came for miles to visit his grave. They entered a cemetery of twenty-five graves through a gate over which is a placard written in Spanish. It reads, "A memorial to Don Pedrito Jaramillo from the Señor Cortez and his Co-operators."

Visitors kneel at his grave and pray; they say the rosary. They bring candles in glass containers, with the figure of the Virgin of Guadalupe printed in colors on the glass, to light and place at his grave; they bring wreaths of artificial flowers and statues; they bring other votive articles of many kinds. All is performed in fulfillment of vows made to the spirit of Don Pedrito or in supplication of his help in the spiritual world.

His grave is covered with a roof supported by four posts. At one end, which is protected by the roof, is a narrow shelf on which are placed the lighted candles. At the other end is a placard with the announcement, "Dedicated by the Center of Psychologic-Studies. Love and affection of McAllen, Texas. 1-13-47."

At the foot of the grave a marble slab has been placed by some grateful follower. On it is engraved, translated:

"Pedro Jaramillo. In recompense of his miracle, I dedicate this stone to his memory."

Among the last of those who visited the grave of Don Pedrito on this Día de los Finados (Day of the Dead) was an old man, Don Doroteo González, with his daughter and three grandchildren. They are among those who have inherited the tradition of Don Pedro Jaramillo. Don Doroteo knew him well; his descendants will remember; they will not forget.

DIONISIO TELLS OF HIS CURES

Dionisio Rodríguez was eighty-five years old when he told me about his memories of Don Pedrito.

I was born on February 28, 1849, and was reared in the town of San Carlos, State of Tamaulipas, Mexico.

On a certain day I left my home on foot and walked something like a hundred miles over the mountains to the city of Victoria, where I joined a body of Porfirio Díaz's soldiers. I enlisted for five years. In those days when one had committed some offence, for instance had killed someone, and he went and enlisted in the army for five years, that freed him from all guilt. At the end of the five years I returned to my home. From there I decided at once to leave for Texas. So, in the year 1882, I crossed the Rio Grande, never again to put foot on Mexican soil.

In the year 1884, I was on Rancho Las Parrillas in Duval County working for the gentlemen Frank and Charlie Graves, who had large flocks of sheep. At this time I was very sick with attacks of headaches. I went to the doctor at San Diego more than once, but he could give me no relief. Then one time when I was sick and was taken to San Diego, a friend asked me why I didn't go to Los Olmos to the curandero who was there. My friend offered to take me to get a remedy.

We started out early in the morning in a buggy and rested during the middle of the day at Las Cabras Ranch. Late that afternoon we reached Los Olmos Ranch and the jacal where Don Pedrito was living with a friend and his wife.

When I saluted the curandero and told him that I was seeking a remedy for the sickness from which I suffered, he took a glass of water and offered it to me. I started to take it with my right hand, but he told me to use the other one.

Immediately after drinking the water I felt a relief through all my body. The curandero told me that for the present nothing more was to be done but that the next morning he would give me another remedy. That night my friend and I stayed in the jacal with Don Pedrito and he invited us to eat with him at his table.

The next morning he asked me how I felt. "Very much better," I replied, saying also that I had slept well for the first time in many nights.

"Well," the curandero said to me, "and now so that your cure may be complete, take these," and he gave me three pills. Then he told me that the next day while traveling from San Diego to Rancho Las Parrillas I should pass over a certain cenizo-covered hill, from which I was to gather plenty of that ash-colored shrub, even though I should spend the night on the road.

Then, he told me, the next day when I reached the ranch I should put the leaves of the cenizo to boil in a large pot full of water and keep the pot on the fire until the water was reduced to one half. Then I should remove the pot, let it cool, and strain the liquid.

He said for me to bathe in this water, first soaping myself well. After the bath, I should wrap myself so that I should perspire. Then I was to take one of the pills; in an hour, the second pill; and in another hour, the last one.

When I bade the curandero good-bye, I offered him twenty-five dollars, but he wouldn't accept it; he said that he made no charges for his services. Finally he accepted, as a present, a smaller amount, but I do not remember how much it was, because fifty years have passed, and this is sufficient time to forget.

Some years passed. I was living with my family in Live Oak County. I became sick of attacks in which I would faint. While alone at work I would fall to the ground and lie there until I recovered consciousness.

One time when I knew someone who was going to see Don Pedrito, I sent and asked for a remedy for the trouble from which I suffered. The remedy was rather unpleasant, but I carried it out. It was that I drink a cup of very strong coffee in the mornings, so strong that it stained the cup, without milk or sugar. I was to do this nine mornings in succession. At the end of the nine mornings, I had no disgust for the strong bitter coffee.

And I regained my health for the second time through faith and the remedies of the curandero of Los Olmos.

AN EARLY MEMORY OF DON PEDRITO

Señora Gertrudis C. de Canales was reared on her mother's ranch, Rancho Santa Fé. She was married on May 19, 1886, to Don Jesús Canales, a brother of Don Andrés Canales, owner of Rancho Las Cabras.

She said that she first saw Don Pedrito at the time of her marriage. He took the opportunity to contact the people who had come to the locality to attend her wedding.

Don Pedrito formed the custom of sending notices to the different ranches to notify the people when to expect him at a particular place so that those who were near by and wanted to consult him could meet him there.

DON JUAN AND DON PEDRITO

Juan García Barrera was the owner of San Pedro Ranch in the County of Starr.

When he was fifty-five years old the following happened to him, as told by his granddaughter, the Señora Concha García de la Garza.

In the year 1887, Juan García was living with his family in Mier, Mexico; only one son, Florencio García Canales, lived on the San Pedro Ranch.

One day Don Juan left his home in Mier on horseback with the object of going to his ranch, and from there on to Corpus Christi, where he had a case in court. Some men had stolen some mules from his ranch, and he was having them prosecuted. He was to travel a long and lonely road.

After he had been on the way for some time and was more asleep than awake on account of the hot August day, his horse stopped suddenly and began to rear with fright. Don Juan saw the road blocked by a coiled rattlesnake; by lashes of his quirt he made the horse sidle by. He continued along his way. After a short distance, his horse stopped again in the same way and for the same reason: there was a coiled rattlesnake in the middle of the road. This happened four or five times.

Finally Don Juan decided to kill the rattlesnake. He got off his horse, approached the snake with his quirt in hand; but when he took careful aim to strike, the snake disappeared and in its place there was only a mound of dirt. Astonished, he mounted his horse and continued the trip to Rancho San Pedro without meeting any more snakes.

The next day Juan García Barrera resumed his trip to Corpus Christi. He passed by Los Olmos Ranch, at which he had relatives. With one of them lived Don Pedrito, in whom Don Juan then had little faith. During his visit at this home, Don Juan said to the curandero, "Listen, Old Wizard, what does this signfy?" And he related what had happened to him with the snakes.

Don Pedrito sat thinking. After meditating for some minutes, he told the man very seriously, "Friend, don't go to Corpus Christi; what you will lose because of the mules will be little compared with what you are going to lose if you continue with the intention of going to Corpus Christi. It is better that you return to your home as quickly as you can."

Don Juan paid no attention to Don Pedrito. He went to Corpus Christi and attended to the business satisfactorily. On his return, he stayed at his San Pedro Ranch some days, where he sold $14,000 worth of horses.

Then he left the ranch to return to his home in Mier. Before he reached the Rio Grande, some men kidnapped him. This was a plan that they had had for a long time. He learned later that once when he had left Mier to go to his ranch these same men had intended to capture him on the road. At this time, before he reached the place where they were waiting for him, a messenger sent from his home caught up with him to tell him that one of his daughters had taken smallpox. He returned quickly without knowing that he had escaped being kidnapped. But on this second time there was no escape. The bandits took him, blindfolded him, and kept him hidden while they opened negotiation with his son. They demanded $25,000 ransom. The son sold the horses, the goats, and all that could be sold from Rancho San Pedro to meet the demand of the kidnappers. The ranch was impoverished. Fifteen days passed; on the sixteenth day the son left the $25,000 with a rich merchant in Roma to pay the agent of the kidnappers. That same day Juan García Barrera, blindfolded and nearly dead from hunger, was delivered to the home of a relative in Roma.

After this experience Don Juan had faith in Don Pedrito.

HOW SEÑORA TOMASITA DE CANALES WAS CURED

IN THE YEAR 1889, Doña Tomasita, the wife of Don Andrés Canales, the owner of the well-known Las Cabras Ranch, in Jim Wells County, became sick of a malignant fever. Señor Canales called a doctor from Corpus Christi, who came and prescribed medicines for her, but she grew no better. Then another doctor was sent for from the same town. He attended her for a few days until he, too, confessed that he had done all that he could, all that science prescribed, and that in his opinion there was no cure for the lady.

Don Andrés then suggested taking his wife to San Antonio, but the doctor said that she would not survive the trip from the ranch to Collins, which at that time was the nearest railroad station. The trip would have had to be made over a twenty-five mile unimproved road by a horse-drawn conveyance.

Let Judge José Canales of Brownsville tell the rest of the story as he wrote it in a letter to me.

While I was not present when my mother was sick, yet

I have heard the account of her sickness and cure both from her own lips and from my father's, especially from my father, who was very accurate in his statements and who was not a believer in Don Pedro as a faith healer until this incident took place. . . .

My grandmother was then alive and attending my mother during her sickness. My mother had lost consciousness. My two brothers, Albino and Andrés, had been sent for from Matamoros, where they were attending school, and my mother was unable to recognize them. When my grandmother was advised what the doctor had said, she suggested to my father that since the doctor had no hope for her recovery and since she (my grandmother) did have faith in Don Pedro Jaramillo's power to cure, he (my father) should send a messenger to Los Olmos and ask Don Pedro for some recipe (*receta*). My father consented and sent a cowboy there, and Don Pedro prescribed that she should be bathed in "natural" water (unheated water) three times, once every two hours. When this message came, the last doctor was returning to Corpus . . . , and he said that if they bathed my mother in cold water she would die. (At that time, according to medical science, when a person had high fever, it was not considered safe to prescribe cold water as an antidote. You know that now doctors often prescribe cracked ice in such cases.) My mother was bathed in cold water according to the prescription sent by Don Pedro, and she survived the ordeal. The first bath was given late in the evening, and the others were given during the night. On the next morning my mother was able to recognize my two brothers.

Don Pedro had sent word by the cowboy that he would come over to our ranch the following morning, which he did. When Don Pedro arrived the next day, my mother had recovered consciousness and was able to recognize and talk to him.

I do not know how long it took her to recover or what other prescriptions were administered by Don Pedro. All I do know is that she got well, and when I came home from college I found that my mother had lost all her hair as the result of the fever. Prior to this fever my mother was of a slender physique, and after this fever she began to put on flesh and continued to be rather stout in physique up to her death.

It is true that my mother had a great deal of faith in Don Pedro, as you naturally would suppose; but it is not true that she never took other medicines or remedies except "In the name of God and of Don Pedro." She was attended by other physicians, and while she was a very religious woman and a good Roman Catholic up to her death, she did not worship Don Pedro in the same sense indicated by some people.

We revere the name of Don Pedro as we think he was God's instrument to save my mother from death at that time, and we still have an enlarged picture made from a kodak which my mother ordered made, but we do not ascribe to Don Pedro any other power except the fact that we believe that he was one of God's humble instruments for good among our people, especially those who hold the true faith in Jesus Christ our Lord.

TOMÁS FLORES HAD NO REGRETS

TOMÁS FLORES, while doing yard work, told me that he was living at the age of seventy-five because first it was God's will and after this because Don Pedrito had cured him.

When he was a youth he was in a very bad state of health as a result of sunstroke. He was living in Yorktown, something like a hundred miles from Los Olmos. It was in the year 1893. At this time a subject of talk in all parts of the country was the marvelous cures that were being made by a curandero, Pedro Jaramillo, who lived at Los Olmos Ranch.

One day Tomás Flores started out on horseback to the place where this man lived to see if he could help him. He was so sick, he said, that he had to travel slowly. When he reached the town of Alice, he was told that the one he was looking for was there making cures. This good luck took something like thirty-five miles off his expected journey.

Tomás joined the crowd that were asking for prescriptions. The remedy for him was that he should go off by himself and bathe nine successive days.

The young man had a hundred ten dollars in his pocket. Of this sum he took twenty-five dollars and made a present to the curandero, who didn't want to accept it; he said he didn't need it, but Tomás made him take it.

Then Tomás started back home, and when he had traveled half of the way he stopped at the town of Beeville, near which was a tank full of water. He stayed there the nine days, going every day to bathe in the tank. He completed the remedy and returned to his home.

The effect of the remedy was miraculous. Never, Tomás Flores said, did he regret the long trip, nor the twenty-five dollars that he had given. He remained as grateful for the cure as he was at the time when it occurred.

THE BEWITCHED WOMAN

Señora Rosa Zamora was born in Corpus Christi, and she has lived there all her life. Now, in the year 1951, when she is bedridden, she recalls a trip she made to see Don Pedrito, like many others from Corpus at that time. She had a reason for wanting to go: Lucinda, her little ten-year-old girl, had a swelling on her neck that she hoped to have the faith healer cure.

She had a compadre who owned a wagon and team. He offered to take her and her little girl, with his wife and several other women who were going with him. Lucinda, apparently, was the only one of the party who needed the services of the curandero, the curer. The others, with the exception of the mother, may have gone in the interest of getting prescriptions for friends or relatives who for some reason were not able to join the pilgrimage themselves; or they may have gone just to make a pleasure trip.

At times a journey of sixty or more miles through the undeveloped open country, which took a week by the slow way of wagon and team, could possess attractions. In the spring this country can be beautiful with shrubs and wild flowers such as bluebonnets, Indian pinks, and many other varieties. Lucinda remembers that it was in the spring when they went.

The Los Olmos Ranch was then a scattered settlement of thatched log huts or jacals, as Doña Rosa described it. And there was not a railroad or a town within thirty-five miles of Los Olmos; the railroad did not come in until 1903.

When this party arrived, there were others there to see Don Pedrito, a young woman with her father and mother among them. The group that included Doña Rosa and her little girl were seated on a bench in Don Pedrito's jacal awaiting their turn to interview him, when the young woman was taken with a seizure of convulsions. Doña Rosa and her friends were frightened. They saw in this attack, according to their belief, a case of bewitchment.

The young woman fell to the dirt floor. She became unconscious; her teeth were clinched; and her face turned black. Her parents carried her and placed her on Don Pedrito's bed. He worked with her, trying to open her mouth. He asked someone to give him a piece of chocolate from a shelf on the wall; with this he rubbed her teeth and gums, but he didn't succeed in reviving her. Then he left her lying on the bed while he gave his attention to the others.

For Lucinda, he told her mother to get a small bottle of olive oil, the kind that sold for ten cents at that time, and to take a chicken feather, dip it into the olive oil and oil the sole of each of her feet with it, from the toes back to the heel, in that order, for nine nights.

What prescriptions Don Pedrito gave the other women, if any, Doña Rosa didn't learn or has forgotten. All of them were so upset over the sight of the young woman that they hurried away as soon as they were able to do so. In fact, Doña Rosa said, Don Pedrito told them that they were not to stay at his place that night, informing them where they could find a suitable camping place along the way.

The supposedly bewitched woman was not cured, as Doña Rosa learned through some source, and later had the misfortune of falling into the fire during an attack of her sickness and being burned to death.

The remedy for the little girl was put into effect as soon as they returned to their home in Corpus Christi, and she began a steady and a quick recovery. In a short time the swelling on her neck had disappeared. She has no trace of it now when she is a well-preserved grandmother.

AN AX IN THE HAND AND FAITH IN THE HEART

PRISCILIANO MARTÍNEZ was born in the year 1858 and was reared in Brownsville, Texas. At the age of thirty he moved to another locality, one that happened to be nearer Don Pedrito at Los Olmos. He lived in that general area the rest of his life, following his work as a woodcutter. At the age of seventy-six he was still working. He told me that when he went into the woods that were dangerous on account of rattlesnakes, he would kneel down and supplicate God and the spirit of Don Pedrito, who protected him in his work; then he would go ahead with so much confidence that he would not even think of snakes.

The old man talked of cures that Don Pedrito had made in his family. He said one time his wife was very sick of a heart ailment. Finally they had consulted six doctors respecting his wife's sickness, and he had spent a great deal of money trying to have her cured. She had reached a very bad condition, and the doctor then treating her said that she couldn't live more than three days. They had thirteen children, and they all were crying, thinking that the hour of their mother's death had come.

At this point Don Prisciliano went to a friend and asked him as a favor to write a letter to Don Pedrito. The curandero replied very quickly. He prescribed that for five nights the señora drink a glass of water recently brought from the river, which was near at hand. She recovered and lived many years afterwards. The cost of the prescription was the ten cents that was enclosed in the letter for the reply; the cost of the doctors' treatments was a hundred dollars.

Another cure was that of Prisciliano's son, Pablo. When Pablo was only a few months old, he became sick. The remedy for him was that his mother put some cold water in a vessel and with a cake of soap between her hands soap the water well; and that in this same water she bathe the baby daily for eleven days. The mother disliked to put the sick baby into the cold water, but she had faith and did as directed. Pablo survived, and when he grew up he became a good vaquero.

Don Prisciliano told of being cured himself. Some heirs of a large ranch were dividing it, and they gave him employment as an overseer of the men who were hauling posts to build the fences. Some of these men resented him as their boss; they attacked him and beat him until he was unable to work. He set out to see Don Pedrito. As he traveled, he felt better. When he reached the presence of the curandero, Don Pedrito told him, without waiting for him to ask for a prescription, that there was nothing the matter with him, that he should return to his house and take a warm bath.

After doing this, the old man said, he got entirely well and continued his work—"with an ax in the hand and faith in the heart."

MABEL SUTHERLAND REMEMBERS DON PEDRITO

WILLIAM SUTHERLAND was a Scottish schoolteacher who taught fifty-five consecutive years along the west side of the Nueces River, first at one ranch settlement and then at another. He taught at Los Olmos Ranch once in the eighties and again in the middle nineties.

His daughter Mabel related to me some of her memories of Don Pedro Jaramillo.

I remember Don Pedrito very well. In the years when my father taught school at Los Olmos Ranch we lived there. Don Pedrito was there at the same time. We considered him a friend.

While my father was teaching the school, he was also appointed postmaster of the newly established post office of Paisano. The family helped him in this work.

The mail was brought in relay once a week from some distance away by a man on horseback. Each time the mail arrived there were letters for Don Pedrito, some of them registered, containing five, ten or more dollars. If a letter came written in English, it was necessary that one of us read it to him, and then write the reply, because the curandero didn't know English. Sometimes when he came for his mail (it was only a short distance) he would stay and talk a while with my father, but he was usually too busy with the people who came to his house to tarry.

At times when my mother was not well and she would ask Don Pedrito to prescribe for her, he would refuse. He would tell her kindly, "I can't cure you; you have no faith." But he did cure me.

One time I had a toothache very badly. I couldn't sleep. I had suffered several days and nights with it. My father decided to take me the thirty miles to a doctor to have him pull my tooth—at that time there were no dentists in that part of the country.

Before we left, Don Pedrito returned. He had been absent from the ranch for some time visiting other places, as was his custom. I was crying with pain. My father said to him, "See if you can do something for this girl to ease her somewhat."

He told me to take a clove of garlic and put it in the hot ashes to roast it; then to put it in the shoe on the opposite side from the tooth that was aching; and to fasten the shoe and not to take it off that night. I carried out the remedy as directed, and we started on our trip.

The pain continued all day. When night came, my father said that we would have to camp so that the horse could rest. For ourselves we expected little rest, judging by the nights we had spent before. Nevertheless, we spread a bed and lay down. I left the shoe on that had the garlic in it. From the moment I lay down, I lost consciousness until at daylight when my father woke me by asking me how my toothache was. I jumped up and said to him, "Do you believe that it no longer aches? The pain is entirely gone."

"I do believe it," he told me, "because you have slept the night through."

We completed the trip that day, and were in the town visiting friends, waiting to see if the toothache would return. It did not, and we didn't go to see the doctor. We went back to the ranch, and the tooth came out in pieces, without any pain, just as Don Pedrito had said it would.

One time when my father was going away for a few days, he told my mother that a paralyzed man who was near by might die before his return, and in that case she was to give some of my father's clothes for his burial. I don't know who the man was or where he came from. It had been a month or more since Don Pedrito had gone on one of his missions, and at this time he returned. He was called at once to see the paralytic. He told those who were there to take him to the creek and throw him into the water. As long as the sick man couldn't walk he was to be put on a *zalea*—a sheepskin with the wool still adhering to it—and dragged to the creek. At the creek, Don Pedrito said, a certain man, who was large and strong, should pick him up and throw him in.

They took him and threw him into the water, fearing that they were going to drown him. The man hardly came out with his life. The second day they took him again, and he came out more easily. On the third day, he could walk a little. On the fourth day they put a chair a short distance from him so that he could walk to it and sit down and rest; they repeated this until he finally reached the creek. Then they threw him into the water, and he came out perfectly well and able to walk without any help whatever.

Once a family came all the way from New York to see Don Pedrito. From the railroad station nearest Los Olmos they had to take a hired conveyance. They were bringing a little paralyzed boy. Don Pedrito was away, so they had to camp out until his return. The father would walk about the place carrying the little boy in his arms.

Finally the curandero came. The parents consulted with Don Pedrito and then left. After some time, they wrote a letter telling him that the little boy had recovered completely. And they sent him a present of two thousand dollars.

Once after I had visited an aunt in Louisiana I returned home sick. I was very nervous; at times I would become hysterical. Don Pedrito saw the condition I was in and told my mother that I should bathe in a tub of water three successive mornings at sunrise. She was to make me a jacket of new unbleached muslin without sleeves and I was to wear this jacket without taking it off until the end of nine days. When all of this was done, I became tranquil and regained my health.

BORROWED SHOES

A MAN who didn't have much faith in Don Pedrito as a healer asked him for a remedy for the malady from which he suffered. The curandero gave him such a simple prescription that the man doubted his power still more. He asked him, "Are you sure this remedy will cure me?"

Don Pedrito assured him, "I am as sure that this remedy will cure you as I am that you are wearing borrowed shoes."

The man was convinced because he *was* wearing borrowed shoes. And all doubt left him when the remedy took effect.

CHAT VELA AND THE BRUJO

CHAT VELA was a dealer in horses and mules. One time when he threw his rope at a horse, he missed the horse and roped a wild mule instead. While he was attempting to get the rope off, the mule kicked him on the shin, halfway between the ankle and the knee. This hurt gave him a great deal of trouble; a large blue spot formed at the place.

When he drove a bunch of horses to market at San Antonio, he consulted the well-known Dr. Herff there. The doctor suggested cutting into the leg and taking out any sliver of bone that might have penetrated into the marrow; this was the nature of the trouble, the doctor thought. But Chat wouldn't consent to the operation.

After he had tried many home remedies, his wife suggested that he go to Don Pedrito, the curandero at Los Olmos. But Chat only laughed the suggestion aside. He knew the curandero, since he made the home of Chat's mother a stopping place on his trips through Live Oak County, where the Vela family lived. Having no faith in his ability to cure, Chat referred to Don Pedro as the old *brujo,* the old wizard.

Then one time when Chat was bringing a bunch of horses

from the Rio Grande country, he and his vaqueros camped one night near the Los Olmos Ranch, where Don Pedrito lived. Chat's leg was hurting him severely. One of the vaqueros suggested that since he was so near the curandero he go to see him. Chat refused at first, but finally gave in.

When he asked for a remedy for his leg, Don Pedrito told him that the leg wouldn't hurt him by the time he got back to camp. But, the curandero said, in order to cure it, Chat should get a porous plaster and put it, not on the left leg—which was the one that was hurt—but on the right leg at the corresponding spot.

Chat was free from pain by the time he got back to camp, as the curandero had said he would be. And at the first opportunity he bought a porous plaster, but didn't use it at once; he still had little faith in Don Pedrito's prescriptions.

Then one time when a relative was visiting the family Chat had a bad spell with his leg. He was suffering so much that the relative urged him to try the porous plaster, and Chat consented.

So while the wife arranged and applied the plaster to the uninjured leg "En el nombre de Dios" (in the name of God) —Chat jokingly pledged: "If that old brujo cures me, I will give him ten dollars and a fine pair of gloves."

The leg got perfectly well. When Chat called on the curandero and presented him with the ten dollars and the gloves, Don Pedrito reminded him, "You are forgetting something."

"What is it, do I owe you something more?" the grateful man wanted to know.

"You should say," Don Pedrito instructed him, " 'Here, old brujo, is ten dollars and a pair of gloves.' "

How did Don Pedrito know that Chat Vela had referred to him as an "old brujo"?

WHEN ONE BRINGS A LIE

IT MIGHT be expected that besides the many people who demonstrated faith, there might be others who demonstrated doubt.

A man in good health thought to prove that Don Pedrito did not have the power that he pretended by asking for a remedy for a sickness that was purely imaginary.

Don Pedrito discovered the fraud. He told the man that in order to recover his health, he must eat a bale of hay.

Then he said to him, "When one brings a lie, he will take a lie."

CURED WITH A LEMON

SALOMÉ RAMÍREZ of Mathis said that he first heard of Don Pedrito when he was a boy living with his family in the town of Realitos.

Late one day an old man, nearly blind, came to their home and asked to stay all night. He was on foot. In those times hospitality was not refused to anyone, not even to a stranger, Salomé said. The old man spent the night with them. He told them that he was going to Los Olmos Ranch to visit a curandero there, to see if his eyes could be cured, because he could see very poorly and was afraid he would lose his sight entirely. He was coming from near Laredo, and had already walked something like seventy miles. The entire trip to Los Olmos would be about a hundred miles. The next morning the old man pursued his journey.

After a time, Salomé doesn't know how long it was, the old man stopped with them again, on his way back to his home at Laredo. And what was their surprise to see him sound and well of his eye trouble!

The Ramírez family later moved to a ranch near the Nueces River. At various times they sent or went to ask for remedies of Don Pedrito for sick members of the family.

The mother, Doña Mariana, was cured of a pain in her side with a poultice made of canned tomatoes. At another time she fell and hurt her leg; this injury was cured with nine baths. Someone else in the family was cured with half a cup of coffee and a tablespoon of whisky.

Salomé said that he got sick and reached such a grave condition of health that he was extremely weak and had fever all the time. An old man who lived a few miles from them used to go to Don Pedrito to get prescriptions for his relatives and friends.

So Salomé asked this old man as a favor, if he were going soon, to get a remedy for him; but the old man was not sure when he would go. Finally when Salomé became very sick, his brother asked him if he thought he could stand the two-day trip to Don Pedrito's. Salomé replied that he wanted to risk it even if he should never reach Don Pedro. So he and his brother started out in a buggy for Los Olmos.

When they had been traveling three or four hours and were going along a narrow road, they met their neighbor, the old man, who was returning from Los Olmos, where he had gone to see Don Pedrito. From a handkerchief in which he had wrapped several prescriptions, he selected the one that pertained to Salomé and gave it to him. With this good luck, the brothers returned to their home. Leaving the sick brother at home, the other brother continued to a nearby town to buy lemons for the prescription.

That night Salomé lay with his feet toward the door. A lemon was roasted, cut in half, and a half put on the sole of each foot.

By the next morning Salomé felt better. At the end of a month, he could come out and get on his horse. And from that time he recovered his health.

WITHOUT LOOKING BACK

THE LATE Harry Timon told me this story.

He said that when he was living on his ranch in San Patricio County, he had another ranch situated on the Rio Grande. When he went to and from this ranch, he passed by Los Olmos Ranch.

At times he would stop there to spend the night with the family of his friend, William Sutherland, who was both schoolteacher and postmaster at Los Olmos. Once when this ranchman was returning from his Rio Grande ranch, on horseback as usual, he was suffering with rheumatism in one leg. He spent the night at Los Olmos.

Before Mr. Timon left the next morning, Mr. Sutherland told him that it would be well if he went and asked Don

Pedrito, who lived near by, for a remedy. Mr. Timon decided to go, but he had to wait some time on account of the many people who were ahead of him, some having come from long distances. Finally he was able to see the healer, who told him that when he started for his ranch in San Patricio he should not turn his head one time to look back in the entire trip of seventy miles. Don Pedrito gave him a piece of cord, telling him to double it in the middle and, while traveling along, to cut it in two with his teeth; then to throw one-half of the cord over his right shoulder and the other half over his left.

His rheumatism got easy, Mr. Timon said.

BATHS AND BEER

ONE TIME when Don Pedrito was returning from Laredo on one of his trips, he met an American and his wife on the road traveling in a buggy. As was the custom with country people in those days, they greeted one another and stopped for conversation.

The man told Don Pedrito that he was taking his wife to Laredo to see whether a doctor could be found there who could cure her. The woman, thin and pale, seemed very sick. The curandero told them that it was not necessary for them to go on to Laredo, for he could cure the sick woman. He told them to return to their home, and to carry out the remedy that he would prescribe for her.

Surely they must have recognized the famous curandero. If he didn't tell them who he was, they could have guessed his identity. His distinguishing marks were too well known over the country not to be recognized; the big felt Mexican hat, the scarred nose, and the long white beard could mean no one but Don Pedro Jaramillo, the curandero.

The couple returned to their home and began to put into effect the prescribed remedy. Each day for nine days, the señora was to bathe in a tub of water, and while in the tub she was to drink a bottle of beer. Before completing the nine days she was so well and so fat that it was feared she would become too fat if she continued taking the baths and the beer until the end of the time prescribed.

The man made a trip to Don Pedrito to ask his advice about this. The curandero replied that they should continue doing as he had instructed them at first, and that when the remedy had been fully carried out the weight of the woman would be normal.

A SURE CURE FOR MIGRAINE HEADACHE

"Yes," José, the young man who was feeding Norman Hoffman's fine horses at San Diego, Texas, said, "I have heard a great deal about Don Pedro Jaramillo."

He went on to say that his parents, who had lived near San Diego for many years, knew him well and depended on him to prescribe for any sickness they might have in the family. But the only remedy he prescribed that José could remember was a cup of water; he had cured them with that only.

It appeared that José didn't care to mention the name of a woman in the family who had severe attacks of migraine headaches. When someone went to Don Pedrito to secure a remedy for her, he sent her word to have her head cut off and thrown to the hogs.

When the woman was told what the curandero had prescribed, she became violently angry—and didn't have any more headaches.

THE GROWTH THAT VANISHED

THE FOSTER family, which included seven children, lived on a ranch about twelve miles from the home of the writer. We were friends.

Mrs. Foster became concerned about herself when a small growth appeared on one of her eyelids and continued to increase in size until it caused the lid to droop. She wanted to go to Corpus Christi, which was the nearest place where the growth could be removed. But the trip with small children and the interrupted travel of horse-drawn conveyance and train were too much for her. She kept putting the operation off, even though she felt that eventually she would have to have the growth removed.

Then one day some member of the family noticed that

the growth had disappeared. To the questions her family and friends asked her in regard to the removal of the growth, she gave the one answer, "Don Pedrito took it off." She never told how she got the prescription, nor what it was. She lived almost a hundred miles from Los Olmos, but not too far for the Mexicans on the ranch to have made the trip to secure a remedy. Mrs. Foster herself may have written Don Pedrito. And she may have been instructed by him not to tell how the cure was accomplished.

In the forty-odd years that she lived after this, she told no one what the remedy was or how she secured it.

AN EPILEPTIC IS CURED

WHEN I first remember Margaret, she was grown and was living with her father and mother in a small town about six miles from the ranch where I was born and reared. She was of mixed nationality; her mother was Mexican, her father American. She was an epileptic, and had been, it was said, from a small child.

A relative of mine told me that when Margaret was a girl, she had her come and stay with her and help with the housework and the care of her children. Margaret's father told this relative not to let his daughter pick up the baby or a lighted lamp on account of the danger of her falling.

One night, my relative said, one of her little girls was sleeping with Margaret when she was taken with a violent seizure of convulsions. This frightened the little girl very badly and convinced the family that Margaret was afflicted.

I never knew Margaret except through other people, and I hadn't heard of her for many years, until I came to live in a small town where she had been living for some time. She was on the streets a great deal, and was helped by several charitable ladies of the town, who saw that she was cared for whenever she was sick. These ladies were surprised when I spoke of Margaret as an epileptic.

Then one time when I was talking to an old woman whom I often visited with, one who told me that she herself had gone to Don Pedrito as early as 1881, it occurred to me to ask her if she knew anyone who had definitely been cured of serious sickness through a prescription of Don Pedrito. She asked me, "Do you know Maggie?" If she meant Margaret Francis, I told her, I had known of her all my life. Later I talked to Margaret, and she told me of her cure.

She said that from the time when she was two years old, at which time she fell out of a swing with the first attack, until she was forty years old, she had suffered from epilepsy. And she was never given any hope of a cure. The sickness kept her in constant peril of being hurt.

The Mexican neighbors were curing themselves with the remedies of Don Pedrito, but since the doctors said that she had no cure, the family didn't approve of her going to Don Pedrito, in whom they did not believe. Margaret, through her faith that Don Pedrito could cure her, sent him a letter asking for a remedy, without letting her family know she had done so.

The prescription the curandero sent her directed her to take a glass of water for nine nights, go out into the yard, raise her eyes to the heavens and say, "In the name of God," then take a taste of the water, and throw the rest out. Margaret did this. From that time on until she died at an advanced age she never had another attack of convulsions.

CURE OF A HORSEBREAKER

SILVERIO RUIZ became a horsebreaker when he was very young. From being hurt so many times in his work with wild horses, he was subject to hemorrhage of the lungs. At times, he said, when a horse would be bucking with him, he would have a hemorrhage that would bathe the horse's shoulders with blood.

Then one time when Silverio and his family were living in the home of his father-in-law, Don Pedrito arrived on his way through that part of the country. Silverio was not at home. Don Pedrito remained for a while and gave prescriptions to different members of the family who needed them.

When he was ready to leave, he bade them good-bye; when he reached the door, he turned and said to them, "All of you have thought only of yourselves, but of the one who is not here and who is more sick than any of you, not one of you has thought. But," he went on, "I am going to leave him a prescription. Tell him to buy a bottle of whisky that sells for twenty-five cents, of the kind that is called '*mataburros*,' and to drink it all at one time."

Silverio said that he complied with the direction and became very drunk. It is no wonder—*mataburros* means "it kills burros." Silverio fell off his horse and remained lying on the ground all night. By the next morning, he felt that he was well; and from that time on he never again had another hemorrhage.

VARIOUS CURES

At times a man suffered from headache until he took to his bed. The remedy for him was that for three mornings he should get up at the same hour and drink a glass of water. He recovered in three days.

For a sick girl, the remedy with which she was cured was that she take a bath every night for nine nights, washing her head well with soap; then that she eat as much as she should want of a can of fruit of whatever kind was available and place the remainder where only the chickens could find it.

The prescription for a certain woman was to dip her head into a bucket of water as she was ready to go to bed. The next morning she was to put half a can of tomatoes into each shoe, then put the shoes on and wear them that way all day, *sin verguenza*—without shame.

A case of particular interest, it was said, was that of a Colonel Toribio Regalo who was brought from the city of Torreón, Mexico. He was so violently insane that he was kept tied. Don Pedrito prescribed a can of tomatoes every morning for nine mornings. The man was confined at Los Olmos while he took the remedy. At the end of nine days he was well, and his friends took him back to Mexico.

A man had a very fine horse that got sick. Don Pedrito told the man to tie the horse to a chinaberry tree at twelve o'clock sharp, and at one o'clock sharp to take him away from the tree. With this the horse would get well and the chinaberry tree would die.

A GRASSBURR IN HIS THROAT

THE WIFE of Don Albino Canales of Premont, Texas, told me a story about a man who lived in Mexico and became very thirsty one day while traveling. He came to a pond and stopped to drink. He drank fast and didn't see the grassburr that was in the water, and it went down into his throat and stuck there.

He went to a doctor, but the doctor couldn't get it out. He went to several doctors, who told him that only through an operation could the grassburr be removed. The man didn't want to have an operation, and he didn't know what to do. He suffered greatly.

At last he resolved to go to Texas to see the famous curandero, Don Pedrito Jaramillo, since he had heard much talk of the difficult cures he was making.

The remedy for the man was to drink all that he could of water with salt in it. He did so. This nauseated him at once and caused him to vomit and expel the grassburr. This burr had sprouted two little leaves.

A CITIZEN OF LEÓN, MEXICO, VISITS TEXAS

AN OLD man wrote me this in Spanish. I translate.

The fame of the cures that Pedro Jaramillo was making having spread through various states of Mexico, a citizen of the town of León, in the State of Guanajuato, started out in search of health, toward the State of Texas, to the Los Olmos Ranch, where Don Pedro Jaramillo lived.

This man suffered with rheumatism and cramps in his legs. The remedy for him was to put on water to heat at midday, and when it was as warm as he could stand it, to bathe in it from his waist down, covering himself with a thick sheet and staying covered as long as he was in the water. When he got out of the water, he was to rub himself with a wool blanket until he was well dried, even to his toenails.

This remedy was to be performed twice, once a day. On the third day the man was well.

THE NAMESAKE IN NEW MEXICO

IN SOCORRO, New Mexico, there lived an American and his wife who had no children. Working for them they had a Mexican family whose young son became sick. They called a doctor, who said that the boy had liver trouble. He prescribed for him, but the medicine did no good. After a time, the doctor decided that the boy did not have liver trouble—what ailed him was tuberculosis.

The American told the boy's parents to move him some distance away from his house, because he was very much afraid of the sickness. There the boy stayed, pale and weak, in bed all the time.

The American went to California, where he remained for a while. His wife did not see the boy for some time. Then one day she was surprised to see a boy that looked like the sick boy running and jumping outside.

She asked a member of the family if it were possible that it could be the sick boy. Yes, was the answer; the boy was now well. When she investigated, the family told her that they had sent to ask a remedy of a Mexican faith healer in Texas, and that with a simple remedy prescribed by this curandero the boy had been cured.

The woman then told them to do her the favor of sending and asking the healer for a remedy for her. The remedy, whatever it was, had such good effect that when her husband returned from California he was surprised to find her in good health as well as the Mexican boy.

The American man wanted to send through the Mexicans a good present of money. But the curandero sent word to wait a year and they could come to see him; and then they could bring something with them.

At the end of the year the Americans came in response to his invitation. But the first thing the man did was to offend Don Pedrito by offering him money.

Don Pedrito told them that he would never again prescribe for them. Nevertheless, the man left him a fine suit of clothes and a gold watch.

The wife had a baby in her arms that had been given

the name of Peter—in honor of Pedro Jaramillo, the Mexican faith healer.

THE NIGHT OF THE NEW MOON

FELIPE LERMA said that once he was sick without knowing what was the matter with him. At that time Don Pedrito came to the town of Beeville, in Bee County, where Felipe lived. He went to consult him. The curandero asked him what his sickness was. Felipe told him that he didn't know, only that he didn't feel well.

Then Don Pedrito told him that what he had was *susto*, fright arising at a certain time and continuing afterwards so as to cause chronic sickness.

"If you don't want to tell the cause," Don Pedrito added, "I shall tell you. There were four men together; one of them killed one of the others and the dead man fell at your feet. At this your heart stopped, and from this resulted your sickness."

And it was the truth that this had happened, Felipe said.

Don Pedrito gave him a remedy. On the night of the new moon, after he had eaten his supper and was about to go to bed, he should take a bottle of beer and empty it into a *jarra*, or some other vessel, and drink it all at one draught. He should do this three times, each time on the night of the new moon.

Felipe said that this remedy cured him of the fright.

FROM THE NORTH

A MAN and his wife arrived from *"El Norte"* at a hotel in the town of Alice, Texas. They had traveled over much of the country for the wife's health, consulting doctors at different places, but they had found none who could cure her.

When they were at the hotel in Alice, someone, in order to entertain them, told them about the famous Mexican faith healer who lived in that part of the country and whom many believed in and consulted. These strangers resolved not to let this opportunity pass to investigate the strange healer. They went the thirty-five miles to Los Olmos to see him.

When the strange woman requested Don Pedrito to do something for her, he asked for a cup of coffee. He took a sip of the coffee, saying, "In the name of God," and then passed it to the patient for her to do the same. In that way, from one to the other, they passed the cup of coffee until they had drunk it all, repeating at each sip, "In the name of God."

In a few days the man and his wife left Alice for their home. Some time passed. Then one day Mrs. Clark, who kept the hotel, received a letter from the man in which he told her that his wife was "sound and well" in health. She had recovered very quickly from the day that they had gone to consult the Mexican faith healer of South Texas.

WITHOUT THE DOCTOR'S KNOWLEDGE

THE SEÑORITA Eduwiges Hernández of Mathis, Texas, was very sick one time when the family lived in the country. Her parents sent to the nearest town to call a doctor. When the doctor came and examined the patient, he said that nothing but an operation could save her life—she could not live more than two days without it. The parents would not give their consent. The doctor became very angry and left, feeling that he had done all that he could under the circumstances.

Immediately, one of the sons was sent, horseback, the seventy miles to get a prescription from Don Pedrito. The patient remained very sick. The son returned as quickly as possible with the remedy that Don Pedrito had prescribed —black coffee and whisky. When administered, it had the desired effect. This was four days after the doctor had made his visit.

The next day the doctor called, thinking, they said, to find that the patient had died. But what was his surprise to find her completely recovered! He wanted to know by what means she had made the recovery, but they never would tell him.

A HOT BATH FOR FEVER

MR. ZACK GORBERT, who when I talked to him lived at Sandia, Jim Wells County, Texas, was working on a ranch, La Coma, in Hidalgo County, when he was a young man.

One time when he was on a certain part of the ranch, he had lodging with a Mexican family by the name of Garza.

When he returned to the house one day in the late afternoon, he found two men there who had come to the ranch to buy mules. One of the men was sick and he occupied Zack's bed while at the house. He stayed there that night, and continued sick with high fever. The next morning they put him in a wagon and took him to another ranch. Zack slept on the bed the sick man had used.

In a few days Zack himself had fever; then one morning he was broken out with measles. Doña Catarina Garza, the housewife, advised him to take good care of himself. She wouldn't give him water to wash his face although he was burning with fever, and would give him only a little water to drink; she was afraid the water would do him harm. But this good woman sent a boy horseback forty miles to ask for a remedy of Don Pedrito.

All that day, all night and the next day, Zack was very sick and restless. By afternoon, he was almost in despair, impatiently awaiting the boy's return with the hope that he would bring him some relief. At last, late in the afternoon, when the sun was almost down, the boy arrived.

He gave the prescription to the señora, who, as soon as she read it, ordered a pot of water put on the fire to get hot, because the remedy was to be carried out at sunset, and it now lacked only a little of that time.

While the water was heating, a large tub made of half a barrel was placed at the side of the patient's bed. Plenty of water, as hot as could be borne, was put into it. Then the sick man got into the hot bath. He felt such a relief that he stayed in for some time. After this he drank all the water he wanted. This remedy was to be performed at sunset on each of three days. After the second treatment Zack was so much better that he was moved to another house, so fully recovered that he didn't require any further treatment.

HALF A GLASS OF TEPID WATER

WHEN JOSÉ Treviño was a boy, he had nosebleed so often that his family were uneasy about him. They thought he might die before the bleeding could be stopped.

One time when an uncle of his went to get a remedy for another member of the family, the mother of José sent to ask for a remedy for him too. Don Pedrito said for him to take, for seven nights, a half glass of tepid water in his left hand, and drink it at bedtime. After taking this remedy, José never, not one time, had another nosebleed. So José told me.

NOSEBLEED

WHEN SIMÓN Valdéz was a boy, he lived on a ranch in the county of Duval. One day Don Pedrito was there giving remedies to those who wanted them. Simón's grandmother asked for a remedy for nosebleed, from which Simón suffered frequently.

The curandero told the grandmother that as a remedy she should put clean clothes on her grandson and not change them for nine days. During this time, every night she should pour a bucket of water over the boy until he was thoroughly wet, and he should sleep that way. Simón said that he didn't feel cold at night with the wet clothes on, although it was in the winter. He was cured of nosebleed from that time on.

THREE LEAVES OF PRICKLY PEAR

IT WAS TOLD that a señora suffered with severe pains in her stomach, which at times caused her to take to her bed. Her husband had called doctors to her at various times when she had these attacks. And not until he was sure that the doctors were not going to cure her of this sickness did he take her to Don Pedrito.

When the woman explained her sickness to the curandero, as the doctors had diagnosed the case, he said, "No, that is not your trouble; it is in your kidneys."

He prescribed that when she had the pains her husband should roast three leaves of prickly pear cactus, slice them through the middle and scrape the pulp out as quickly as possible so as not to lose the heat. Of this warm pulp he should make three poultices, placing the pulp between pieces of muslin. Then he should fix a poultice over each kidney and a third one over the stomach, so that the one over the stomach was in line with the ones over the kidneys.

This señora was entirely cured, it was said.

ESCAPE FROM A MAD DOG

A FAMILY with a sick child camped one night near a lake before reaching Los Olmos. They expected to complete the trip early the next morning. That night they lay on the ground to sleep. About midnight the man awoke frightened, without knowing why. He continued restless and nervous, with a feeling of urgency to get away from that place, to reach their destination as soon as possible.

He awakened the rest of the family and had them get up. They started for Los Olmos at once. When they reached Don Pedrito, the man asked his pardon for disturbing him so early in the morning, and related what had occurred to him. Don Pedrito explained to him that this signified that a mad dog would have bitten him if he had stayed there a little longer.

This was confirmed when, on their return to the place where they had camped the night before, they saw a dead dog that someone had killed after they had left.

The sick child bathed in the lake, which was the remedy that Don Pedrito had prescribed for it, and the family took the road for home, very thankful that they had had the good fortune to escape from the mad dog.

THE CURE OF A HORSE

MARIANO RAMÍREZ did not own a horse. At a time when most of the men in the part of Texas where he lived were on horseback, he was afoot. He wanted to buy a horse but he could never save enough money. One day, he said, he went to a ranch where he had seen a horse that looked good but that had been overheated at some time and was wind-broken.

It occurred to Mariano that the manager of the ranch might sell the horse very cheap because he couldn't be used in the work on the ranch. Mariano's idea was to buy the horse and then cure him.

First the manager asked sixteen dollars. Mariano had only fourteen dollars, which he offered, saying he could pay no more. The manager accepted, and Mariano took the horse home.

The next day he wrote a letter to Don Pedrito, asking for a remedy and sending a dime for the reply. Mounted on the horse, he went very slowly six miles to the post office to mail the letter. When he arrived, the horse was "rocking" from the exercise. Mariano got off and tied his horse in the shade of a tree, where he left him for some time to rest before making the return trip.

In a few days, Mariano received the reply to his letter. Don Pedrito told him to tie the horse where he could get neither water nor anything to eat for three nights in succession, but during the day to permit him to have all the water and feed that he wanted.

Mariano did as instructed. The horse recovered and served him well for a long time.

MYSTERIOUS MONEY

An old woman who peddled various sorts of ware told me a story that another woman had told her.

A very poor woman went to Don Pedrito and asked for a prescription. He told her that she was not sick, that poverty was all that ailed her. He said that he would relieve her of this, but that she must not tell anyone, neither father, mother, brother, nor sister. And so it was that money came into her possession without her knowing how. Her sister became suspicious and threatened to punish her severely if she didn't tell her how she was receiving the money. She had to reveal that she was kept supplied through the power of Don Pedrito.

The next time she went to her trunk to get the money she expected to find there, there was none. And she never again received money from this source.

All night Monico remained on his canvas bed,.
rocked by the movement into a pleasant sleep.

THE MARVELOUS CURE OF A SHEPHERD

MONICO HINGUANZA was a shepherd who had been sick for some time. He took various home remedies, but they did him no good, and instead of getting better he grew worse.

His friends told him of the cures that Don Pedrito had made, and they advised him to go to the curandero. But as Monico lived sixty miles from Los Olmos, he thought it too difficult to make such a long trip.

Finally, when he found that he had to get help, he borrowed a horse and started out for Los Olmos Ranch and Don Pedrito. He reached there the second day at dark. It had rained and the creek was swollen; Don Pedrito's hut was near the bank.

When Monico asked him for a remedy, Don Pedrito got up and took a piece of heavy canvas and a pillow. Telling the shepherd to come with him, he took him to the edge of the creek, where the water made an eddy. He threw the canvas into the eddy, which caught it and extended it in the turn of the water; then he tossed the pillow onto the canvas. The curandero then picked up Monico and placed him also on the canvas, which instead of sinking supported him. All night Monico remained on this canvas bed, rocked by the movement into a pleasant sleep. In the morning Don Pedrito came and took him out of the water, sound and well.

Monico was so thankful that he made Don Pedrito, who had never married and had no family, a present of one of his boys, to live with him and serve him in all that he might command.

CURED OF DRINKING

JOSÉ C. LOZANO, postmaster at Concepcion, told this about his uncle, who was the mail carrier from Concepcion to Los Olmos.

This uncle was addicted to drink, José said. He asked Don Pedrito for a remedy to make him quit drinking. The curandero told him to bathe three days in succession in the water tank that was near his house. Don Pedrito's knowledge that there was a tank near the man's house was a manifestation of his clairvoyant power, it was thought. José's uncle took the three baths as directed.

Then in a few days as he was going down the road, he met a friend who offered him a drink. He took the bottle of whisky and raised it to his lips; but he felt such a repugnance for it that he couldn't swallow.

For the fifty years he lived after that, he never again took a drink of whisky.

DON PEDRITO SINGS

Don Pedrito didn't have a good voice for singing, and he didn't care to sing when he thought that someone might hear him. But there were times when he traveled at night, surely with a heart full of peace and good will and perhaps gayety also, that he would lift up his voice and announce himself when he was least expected to.

One dark night when he traveled towards home he passed close to a place where some people were camped. Because of the darkness, he didn't see them, but they didn't fail to hear him singing.

The man in the party called to the singer and asked him if they were on the road that led to Los Olmos.

"Yes, sir," the singer informed him. "Are you going to Los Olmos?"

The man explained that they were taking a sick person to the curandero who lived there. He asked if the singer knew whether the curandero was good or not.

"No," Don Pedrito responded, "I don't know whether he is good or not; but I do know that right now he is mounted on this horse."

AT MIDNIGHT IN A LAKE

Mr. J. Frank Dobie told me that the Mexicans on his father's ranch in Live Oak County used to take as long as a week to visit Don Pedrito. Among them was a vaquero, Antonio de la Fuente, who had asthma very badly.

Don Pedrito told him to ride into a lake at midnight to where his horse would be swimming and he would be completely wet; then to come out and go to a house and wrap himself up, without taking off his wet clothes, not even his *chivarras*—his leather leggings. Thus wrapped up, he was to go to bed and stay until he was perfectly dry.

What effect this treatment had on the vaquero's asthma, Mr. Dobie doesn't know, but he does know that Antonio worked for his father many years after that time.

BOWLEGS

WHEN MIGUEL RUIZ was a small child his legs were so bowed that the other children of the family laughed at him. His grandmother would say that he was going to be a good vaquero because he already had the right kind of legs.

The boy continued bowlegged until he was about five years old. One day when Don Pedrito was calling at the home of this family, he took notice of him playing outside. He called him, and when he came to him, he stretched him on the ground, and gave him a tap on each leg with the back of his closed pocket knife.

From then on Miguel's legs began to straighten, and it became a matter of surprise to the neighbors to see him with his legs perfectly straight.

THE CRIPPLE

A MAN brought his son, crippled since birth, to Don Pedrito to see whether he could give him a remedy that would help him. The boy was able to get around only by dragging his body with his arms.

Don Pedrito told the man that for six nights he should put a wool blanket in hot water, take it out and wring it quickly, and then wrap the boy in it, with his legs perfectly straight. In the morning the father was to unwrap him and take him by the arms and hold him standing straight no less than five minutes each time. Don Pedrito said that the boy would be well in six days, but that before getting up the last day he was to have his entire body rubbed with a sheet as warm as he could stand it.

On the seventh day the boy began getting around like a child that was beginning to crawl. The healer told the father that little by little the boy would straighten his body until he walked perfectly.

The boy recovered entirely, and when he grew to manhood he was completely normal, it was reported.

DIEGO WAS CURED

THROUGH some means Diego was cured; he gave credit to Don Pedrito.

Diego, a little Mexican boy, was born with clubfeet, on the ranch of the writer's brother-in-law, Joe Reynolds, in northern Duval County. This was an out-of-the-way place, and automobiles had not yet come into use. There seemed to be nothing that could be done to remedy the condition of the little boy; it appeared certain that he would be a cripple all his life.

When he was old enough to walk, he could only hobble about. When the other children played and ran, it was pitiful to watch the little cripple try to join them.

The family moved away when Diego was about four years old, but apparently they didn't move very far.

Then a few years later, when I was at my sister's home, I went with her and her husband to a Mexican village ten miles away in which there was a small store. My sister and I were sitting in the store waiting for her husband to get ready to return to the ranch.

A little boy about seven years old came in carrying a gallon oil can. He stood at the counter to be waited on. My sister recognized him and exclaimed to me, "That is Diego; look at his feet!" They were straight, with the tops and sides still showing the effects of having been walked on.

She then asked the boy in Spanish, "Diego, who cured your feet?"

He replied timidly, "Don Pedrito."

"How did he cure you?" my sister wanted to know.

"Quién sabe?" the boy replied in the vernacular.

He didn't know or didn't want to say.

THE SPADE AND THE HOE

THE WIFE of Tomás Treviño was reared at Rancho Davis, on the Rio Grande.

She said that at various times members of her family went from there to consult Don Pedrito, or they sent to get prescriptions. When she took sick of a stomach ailment, in which she felt suffocation, he prescribed that for nine nights she should put a glass of water at the head of her bed, and that the next morning she should drink it "In the name of God." With this treatment she recovered.

Once, on the way to Los Olmos, the family stopped to spend the night with a relative. This relative had a daughter who was in poor health. She joined them to visit Don Pedrito too. When he saw the girl, he shook his head and murmured, "The spade and the hoe. But," he added, "so that the mother will have some consolation, I'll send her a remedy." He prescribed some baths for the girl.

In a short time the daughter died, as Don Pedrito had implied she would.

At another time, the wife of Tomás Treviño had a pain in her side. The remedy for this was that for nine nights, at bedtime, she should wet the soles of her feet with water, and then she should soap them well and leave them that way all night. She did this and recovered from the pain.

Her mother had an eruption under one arm that lasted for a long time. She was unable to dress herself completely, because she couldn't endure a sleeve on that arm. When she consulted the curandero about this ailment, he told her to do nothing for a term of nine months. And at the end of that time, if she was still alive, she was to take a bath daily for nine days and to apply, with a feather, a certain ointment which was very difficult to secure. Finally, Señora Treviño said, they were able to secure the ointment (its name she didn't remember), and at the end of the nine months her mother used it, as Don Pedrito had ordered, and was cured completely.

TO BE WELL IN MARCH

When Ponciano García was fourteen years old, his parents, who had been cured with remedies of Don Pedrito in times past, decided to send him to the curandero to see if he could be cured of catarrh, with which he had been sick almost all his life.

A neighbor family made the trip in a wagon and Ponciano went with them on horseback. It was in the summer time and they spent two days on the way.

When they presented themselves with the crowd that were asking for prescriptions, they saw Don Pedrito, who was standing outside in front of them. In a short time he fixed his attention on the boy. Lifting his hand toward him he said, "December will pass, and by March you will be well." That was all he said to him.

The boy returned to his home. The months passed until March came, the month in which Ponciano became fifteen years old. By this time he was perfectly well, without having taken notice of when he recovered.

From that time on until he died years later, he never was sick of the trouble of which Don Pedrito had cured him.

GOD CURED HIM

DON PEDRITO said that he was not God—there had to be those whom he could not cure. But when someone came to him for whom there was no earthly help, he disposed of him kindly.

A sick man made a painful trip of a hundred miles on horseback, with the last hope of being cured. When Don Pedrito saw him, he told him to return to his home at once. Don Pedrito directed that he and his horse be well fed before starting back and that he be given whatever food he would need for his journey. But he gave him no remedy. He told him that by the time he should reach his home, God would have cured him of all his ailments.

Near his home, the man was found dead by the roadside. God had cured him.

ASTHMA FOR LIFE

AN OLD woman, Agustina de Ibáñez, lived in the town of San Diego, Texas. She had suffered with asthma from the time she was two years old.

During his life Don Pedrito prescribed many times for

her for different sicknesses, but for the asthma he would never give her a remedy.

He said that she shouldn't have a remedy, that as she was so must she continue all her life. He told her that the malady did her more good than harm; and that is the way it appeared, for this woman reached a very advanced age. But she was never free from attacks of asthma.

COMPLETE BUT FOR ONE SON

Doña Ramona Garza and her family, except for one son, were living at a place called Charco, near the San Antonio River in Goliad County.

The woman lost her mind. Her husband went to Los Olmos to consult Don Pedrito to see whether he could help her.

Don Pedrito told him to take the entire family to the San Antonio River, and here they should all go into the river and bathe together. They did this, all except the one son who was away from home and whom they did not know how to reach.

The woman recovered her reason, but not entirely; it was seen that the cure was not complete. This was thought to be the result of the absence of the one son when the others bathed together in the river.

Since the family was not complete, the cure was not complete either.

NOT A TURKEY EGG

A ranchman, Mr. Pete McNeill, lived at a place named Dinero, on the Nueces River in Live Oak County, Texas. He had been sick for some time and could not find a treatment that benefited him, so he decided to ask Don Pedrito for a prescription at a time when he was visiting the Dinero part of the country. The remedy Don Pedrito prescribed was that for nine mornings, before breakfast, Mr. McNeill take a raw egg directly from the shell.

He did this for eight mornings, but on the ninth he had no hen's egg and substituted a turkey egg. Thus he finished the treatment. When he didn't recover from his sickness, he attributed the failure to his having substituted the turkey egg.

A VAQUERO WHO FAILED TO FOLLOW DIRECTIONS

ONE TIME when a vaquero was running some horses through mesquite brush, a limb struck him in the face with such force as to hurt his eyes very badly. He doctored his eyes with different home remedies in vain. Then he sent to ask Don Pedrito for a remedy.

The remedy that Don Pedrito prescribed was that this vaquero should do hard work for nine successive days; that he work with an ax every day, from early in the morning until night; that he take no siesta, nor rest during the day; and that he make no charges for his work.

The vaquero followed directions until Sunday came; but instead of continuing the work on this day also, he rested. The consequence was that he was blind the rest of his life.

FAITH HEALED HIM

THE WOMAN who runs a tortilla factory in San Diego, Texas, said that her father, Marcelino Saenz, had trouble with his teeth, which were in a very bad condition. There were no dentists in the part of the country where he lived; so he went to Don Pedrito and asked for a remedy. Don Pedrito told him to cut up an onion, put salt on it, and eat it for each of nine days.

On the first day, the salt and onion were very painful. The next day when he prepared the onions and salt, he found the remedy so difficult to take that he couldn't force himself to. So he pronounced, "In the name of God," as instructed, but instead of eating the remedy, he threw it over his shoulder. He did this the following seven days. His teeth ceased hurting him, and all of them fell out, one by one.

When he saw Don Pedrito, he told him that he was cured. Don Pedrito told him that he hadn't carried out instructions but that nevertheless his faith had worked a cure.

SOLDIER HERB

ONE DAY three men and a woman came to the house of Don Lino Treviño at Los Olmos. These were three brothers and a sister. One of the men was very sick; he was yellow even to the white of his eyes, and he was full of sores. They asked for Don Pedrito. Don Lino told them that he could give them accommodation at his house and then he would take them to see the curandero, who lived a short distance away.

These people had come from Guanajuato, Mexico, and were traveling in a very good carriage. They had brought a trunk that they guarded with such care that Don Leno told them to put it in a certain room of his house entered by no one but his own family.

Don Pedrito came out of his house and met them before they arrived. He did not usually disturb himself in this manner.

He told the sick man that he had passed his remedy on the road. He told him to gather some of the *yerba del soldado* (soldier herb) that grew about the place and boil it in plenty of water to make a strong brew, and afterwards to bathe in this from head to foot without soap. Don Pedro said that it was not necessary to return to him, but that if one of the brothers wanted to come and let him know how he was getting along, that would be all right. They went back to the house of Señor Treviño.

A brother-in-law of his who knew the soldier herb went out and gathered a lot of it and put it in a large *olla* and made the brew. That night the sick man bathed in this. The next morning he was much better. In three days he was entirely well of the sores and had a good color.

Before going back to Guanajuato, Mexico, the grateful visitors gave the brother-in-law ten dollars for a sack full of the soldier herb that he had gathered for them.

SUSTO CURED BY SUSTO

IT IS TOLD that a youth presented himself to Don Pedrito asking for a remedy. He said that he had a case of *susto* or fright.

The faith healer told him that in order to recover from the effect of this fright, he would have to experience another. The youth was not satisfied; he didn't see how he could arrange to have another fright.

He mounted his horse and took the road for home. Don Pedrito ordered his own horse saddled immediately. He disguised himself in the garb of a bandit. Then putting on his big sombrero and mounting his horse, he started out in the boy's direction, but in a roundabout way so that he would come into the road ahead of him. Here he turned and came back towards the boy. When the boy raised his eyes and saw himself faced with a highwayman, his heart seemed to stand still. He started to turn and put spur to his horse, but he realized that he would be going in the same direction as the bandit. He looked to the right and to the left, but there was no hiding place in the open country. He stopped and stood like a statue in the middle of the road, while the "bandit" came nearer and nearer, presenting a sinister and threatening appearance to the imagination of the youth. He was truly scared. And not until Don Pedrito confronted him with a wide grin, did the youth recognize him. The boy was too shaken to smile back.

"Now," Don Pedrito said as he rode past, "you have had your remedy."

NINE ONIONS AND NINE BATHS

Mrs. Minnie Alexander, who lived in San Antonio at the time, said that Don Pedrito was there around 1895 making so many cures that the papers gave an account of them each day. This woman was in bad health. She resolved to go to see if the unique healer could cure her. She found him on the edge of town, surrounded by people. Through an interpreter, he asked her what her sickness was. She told him that it was that she became very weak with the slightest exertion. He prescribed a remedy which seemed so difficult that Mrs. Alexander thought it impossible to take.

Nevertheless, she stopped at a store on her way home and selected nine onions, not too large; they were to be part of the remedy. Another part was cold baths. These she thought she couldn't take because even her customary tepid baths gave her such chills that she had to wrap herself in a blanket until she got warm.

But she risked the treatment. For three mornings, she ate one of the onions without salt or water. Each time she did this, she became very nauseated. Following this, for three mornings, she took a cold bath. She would leave a tub of water outside all night, according to directions, and at daylight would bring it into the house and take a bath in it at once. The first time, she got into the cold water very slowly, in fear that she would have a chill. But she experienced no bad effects whatever; on the contrary, she found the bath pleasant. And she felt so well that she dressed and went for a walk in the city.

After the three days in which she took baths, she took onions for another three days; and so on alternately until she had eaten nine onions and taken nine cold baths. When this course was finished, she found herself in excellent health.

LITTLE PETRA

Doña Encarnación de Gutiérrez said that she would never forget Don Pedrito. She told me something of her experience with him.

She said that the first time she saw him was in San Diego, Texas, in the year 1902. Being very kind to children, he talked with her. She told him that she was ten years old, and that she was ready to make her first communion.

"That is very well; may your communion be happy," the old man said to her.

This woman married very young, in the year 1906. Her husband told her of a cure Don Pedrito had made for him the year before. He told him to take *Flor de Agosto* (Flower of August) for nine days for his stomach trouble. This cured him.

Then Doña Encarnación became sick. Her husband took her the thirty miles or more to Los Olmos in a wagon with a pair of mules hitched to it. They were two days on the road. When they arrived, she was very sick. With just a glass of water taken "In the name of God" that the curandero prescribed, she recovered. This was the year before Don Pedrito died. He died in 1907.

In the year 1910, this señora made a vow to the spirit of Don Pedrito that if she should maintain good health through a certain time, she would dedicate a child to him. When the baby girl was born it was astonishing to see that she had on her nose a scar similar to that on Don Pedrito's. They gave her the name of Petra, in honor of Don Pedro Jaramillo.

THE CHURCH BELL

SHORTLY BEFORE the time when Pedro Jaramillo came to live at Los Olmos Ranch, then in Starr and now in Brooks County, the French priest, Father Peter Bard, came to live in the adjoining county of Duval, at the small Mexican town of San Diego, Texas.

This saintly priest was destined to cover, for forty years or more, much of the same territory gone over by his namesake Don Pedro. They each made long, lonely, and sometimes dangerous journeys through thinly populated country, Don Pedrito on horseback, Father Bard on horseback at first and then later in a buggy drawn by two horses. They each traveled through the hot summers and the cold winters, over the flower-covered hills and prairies of spring, and through the calm days of autumn. And always they had the same object—to respond to the call of humanity.

Surely it must have been that in the many years when the two were going about in the exercise of their work they would sometimes meet. It would be difficult to think that this had never happened.

In a comparison of these men, the great contrast would appear in their formal education. The priest was of superior education, a scholar; the curandero had very little learning.

After this, the two were of a simple and sincere character. Each went his way without interfering in what did not concern him. Each had the respect and friendship of all who knew him, of whatever nationality or religion. And surely each had the respect of the other.

Señor Lino Treviño, who lived at Los Olmos during the curandero's time, told of a bell in which Father Bard and, later, Don Pedro were interested. He said that when the town of Falfurrias was founded in 1903 it seemed well to the priest that the men of the neighborhood get together to build a church there. In that case he could go directly to the church instead of to the ranches as he had been doing.

The men got together at the restaurant of a woman in Falfurrias to determine how they could build the church. At the close of the meeting each man had pledged to pay his part of the lumber costs. Mr. Jim Allen, who was a carpenter from the town of San Patricio, offered to build the church free of charge, provided that he were furnished two or three helpers.

The church was built. Well, said the señora of the restaurant when she looked at the completed building, how will a church do without a bell? The men hadn't thought of a bell, and they hadn't counted on this extra cost. They went to Father Bard, who showed them a catalog of bells from two hundred dollars up. They decided to go out among their friends to try to collect enough money to buy one of the cheapest bells.

They thought to start first with Don Pedrito to see whether he would be interested in the bell. Don Lino Treviño was commissioned to go to him. He felt a delicacy in doing this, since Don Pedrito was his neighbor and he didn't know how the idea would strike the old man.

He went and told him of the plan they had and asked for a donation. Don Pedrito inquired how much the bell would cost. Don Lino told him that the cheapest one was two hundred dollars.

"How much has been collected?" he asked.

"Nothing," Don Lino told him; "we have just started."

"Well," said the curandero, "don't bother yourselves further. I will give you whatever is necessary. Select the one you want, up to the sum of fifteen hundred dollars, which I shall place at your disposal."

So it happened that for many years the good Father Bard called the faithful of Falfurrias and the neighborhood to church with the bell donated by his namesake, Don Pedro Jaramillo, the faith healer of Los Olmos.

FROM THE TOWN OF REFUGIO

SEÑORA PETRA Rocha de Hernández lived in Refugio. She was born and reared there about one hundred miles from Los Olmos Ranch, where Don Pedrito lived.

He used to visit Refugio when he went about over the country to make his cures. But at the time of Doña Petra's treatment, he was of such an advanced age that he no longer left home. This was only two or three years before his death.

Doña Petra had been married seven years without having any children; she was not in good health and she resolved to consult Don Pedrito. She was taken on the long trip in a wagon. When she presented herself to Don Pedrito, he said to her before she told him the object of her trip, "I know what you came for, and I am going to give you a remedy that afterwards will be a burden; but don't say, 'That old man this, and that old man that.' "

He prescribed that she take a bath in natural water (unheated water) every day for three days at sunset and to throw out the water that remained, not using it for anything else. The señora did this. The next year she had a son, who grew to manhood, married, and had a family. The señora had two more children, a boy and a girl, both of them in perfect health.

When Doña Petra feels sick, she takes her remedies, "In the name of God, and in the name of Don Pedrito," and she said that while she lives she will continue to take them in that way.

THE VOW FULFILLED

ANTONIO PÉREZ, who lived in San Diego, Texas, some years ago, was sick of dropsy, which caused his body to swell. The man was in a very bad state. He went to a curandera, a woman folk doctor, who knew something of the medicinal value of plants and herbs.

The curandera took the leaves of prickly pear, scorched the thorns off; then split the leaves open and scraped the pulp out. Of this warm pulp, she made poultices and bound them on the patient's body. At the same time she made a vow to the spirit of Don Pedrito that if the man recovered his health, she would have a Mass said for him, and she would also put a wreath of flowers on his grave on All Souls' Day.

The man regained his health rapidly.

The Mass was said for the repose of the soul of Pedro Jaramillo at St. Francis' Church in San Diego. And those who, as usual, visited the grave of Don Pedrito at Los Olmos on All Souls' Day might have seen among the flowers there the wreath that had been brought thirty-five miles in fulfillment of a vow.

THE SPIRIT OF DON PEDRITO GIVES HOPE

Señora Eufemia P. de Lemos told me about an appeal that she had made to Don Pedrito's spirit for comfort and support in a time of danger.

In the spring of 1926, when she was living in Mathis, Texas, she and her son became involved in a murder trial. She had innocently rented a room in her house to a strange Mexican who had later helped an American bury the body of a doctor murdered by the American. When the Mexican was traced to her house, she and her son were both arrested. Let her continue with the story.

The officers took me to the town jail, and they took my son and the stranger to Sinton, where they put them in the county jail. I stayed that day in jail.

When I came out, I learned that the strange man had been brought from Laredo, that he had confessed that he, instructed by the American, had come to call the doctor on a pretended case; that the American had killed him and that together they had buried him. The Mexican showed where the body was buried.

The next day I went to Sinton to see my son, and I went almost every day of the fifteen days that they had him in prison. I was nearly crazy; I didn't eat, I didn't sleep; from one day to another, as I visited my son, I felt that I shouldn't find him there, although I knew full well that he was completely innocent.

Some of my friends and relatives advised me one way, others another. I decided to go to San Diego to talk to a lawyer there in whom I had much confidence and who spoke Spanish well. The lawyer advised me to do nothing, saying that with time all would be cleared.

That evening, when I was in the home of my sister, various friends of the town came to give me consolation, but I was disconsolate, seeing no way out of this grave situation.

"Don't be without comfort," said one of my friends. "In this town are a woman and her husband who are spiritualists. They may be able to help you."

This friend took me to the house of the spiritualists. The man asked me what it was I wished to know. I told him that I wanted to know how my son and I were going to come out of this affair in which we found ourselves involved. Then the man asked if there was any certain spirit with whom I wanted to speak. I thought and replied, "I want to speak with the spirit of Don Pedrito Jaramillo."

The man took a piece of paper from a tablet and put it between two little boards attached to a machine sitting on the table. I saw that there was nothing written on the paper when he put it in. He told me to ask whatever I wanted.

I came close to the table and said, "Don Pedrito, do me the favor to tell me how my son and I are going to come out of this business in which we are enwrapped."

The paper moved and came out of itself.

I picked it up and read this: "DO NOT FEAR YOU AND YOUR SON ARE GOING TO COME OUT WELL AND WITHOUT COST PEDRO JARAMILLO."

Well! This took a great weight from my heart. I was consoled, and I had faith that this was a message directly from the spirit of Don Pedrito.

The next day after I returned from San Diego, I went to see my son. I encouraged him to have comfort and faith that we were going to come out well in the end.

For four years, from time to time, we had to go to the courts, first to one place and then to another. At the end of the trial of the American, the court was in a town so strange that no one showed friendliness for outsiders. Even the courthouse, so large and handsome, gave rise to fear and horror. Until the Mexican from Laredo was finally imprisoned, we were not free from this terrible business.

And there was not one of those disgraceful days, so full of fear, shame, and mortification, on which I did not supplicate God to protect us, not one on which I did not pray that the spirit of Don Pedrito, as he had helped us in his mortal life, would also help us, with the power of God, in his spiritual life.

SEÑORA MARÍA SAENZ

SEÑORA MARÍA Saenz of San Diego, Texas, has a large picture of Don Pedrito hanging in her house, and she is taking medicine that is put up by Fernando M. Tijerina, of Laredo, Texas, under the trade-mark "Don Pedrito," with the picture of Pedro Jaramillo and the legend "Supplier of Herbs, Roots, etc." on the container.

This woman had a son in the Army in World War II. She made a vow to the spirit of Don Pedrito that if her boy came back without having to go overseas she would place a wreath on his grave of the value of ten or fifteen dollars.

At three o'clock one morning there was a knock at the door. It was her son. He had been discharged and sent home after three months, without having to go overseas.

Doña María was happy to take a handsome wreath and place it on the grave of Don Pedrito. She had known him well; she had gone to him when she heard he was dying; and she had been at Los Olmos for his funeral.

DON PEDRITO'S SPIRIT IN MONTERREY

THE FIFTEEN-YEAR-OLD Alicia Llorente, who works in the bakery shop of her uncle and aunt, came with them from Mexico to Texas in 1948.

Her aunt said that she had never seen Don Pedrito, since she was not living in this part of the country during his lifetime, but that she had gone many times to a spiritualist center in Monterrey where the curandero's spirit had been called up, from which she had received much help.

Young Alicia volunteered a description of this spiritualist center.

She said the building was a large room fitted with seats, "something like a church." And those who wanted to communicate with a spirit took front seats. The medium, a woman, sat in front in a low chair. She had two helpers, a man and a woman. Their office, Alicia said, was to prevent undesirable spirits from intruding. When the audience had gathered, the door was closed and locked. No one must come in or go out, since that might give an opportunity for bad spirits to come in.

One could entreat, mentally, any spirit he chose, but Don Pedrito's spirit was the most popular. His large picture hanging on the wall, with a votive candle burning before it, was a strong suggestion to most of the applicants to make him their choice. Many did, and felt that they were helped through his messages from the spiritual world.

THE STRANGER AT THE GRAVE

IT WAS All Souls' Day of 1950. People had come and gone all day at the little cemetery where Don Pedrito is buried, and at the larger one across the creek that belonged especially to Los Olmos Ranch.

The sun was nearly down. A small car drove up and passed the entrance gate, then stopped. A young woman got out of the car, walked back to the gate and came in, and crossed to Don Pedrito's grave. She held the usual glass with the votive candle in it and the picture of the Virgen de Guadalupe, the patron saint of Mexico, on one side, and the picture of the Virgen de San Juan de los Lagos on the other side. She stood at the graveside, took a match from the box she held in her hand, struck it and lit the candle, and placed it alongside the others on the shelf put there for that purpose.

The fretful crying of a baby could be heard from the car she had left. She bowed her head in the silent prayer she was offering. Then I, the only other person in the cemetery, addressed her. She indicated that she didn't understand English; then we spoke in Spanish. She said that she was lighting the candle for her sick baby. It was cutting teeth and was having a very bad time. The little mother seemed sad and worried. One might have wondered who was caring for the baby, whether a young husband or some friend who, through sympathy, had brought her here stealthily.

"Do you believe in this?" she asked with an appeal for assurance in her voice.

"I don't believe," I said, "and I don't doubt, but many most certainly do believe."

"My people don't believe in this," she confided. Then she told her story.

Her home had been in Monterrey, Mexico. She had come to this place to visit a friend, had married a young man of the neighborhood, and was now living here. The impression she gave was that it was her husband's people who were not in sympathy with her faith in Don Pedrito. And, yes, she had known of Don Pedrito while she was in Mexico, she said. There is a spiritualist center in Monterrey, she explained, where the spirit of Don Pedrito can be called up and consulted.

She had come in her faith to stand by the curandero's grave and ask his help for her baby.

Don Pedrito has not been forgotten by those who are in need and have faith.

COPIES OF WRITTEN PRESCRIPTIONS

An old woman, Doña Pilar, went into her trunk and brought out these prescriptions and gave them to me. They were written very crudely. Where they are now I do not know; I think I gave them away. I translate from Spanish.

———

Senor Feliciano: Bathe seven nights, at whatever hour you choose, entirely nude, soaping yourself in cold water; have no guard.

———

Don Feliciano, in the name of God, this remedy is for

both of them. Each one take a cup of cumin tea without sugar for seven nights at bedtime.

I received your kind gratuity, for which God will repay you with good health and a good future.

————

Don Feliciano, in the name of God, take a cup of cold water seven nights at bedtime.

Do nothing for the horse; with the favor of God, of a sudden he will recover.

————

Don Feliciano, in the name of God; your wife and your mother should each take a cup of cold water seven nights at bedtime.

A BACKWARD GLANCE

WHAT DO I, the collector and writer of these stories that are told of Pedro Jaramillo, think of the man and his work? I never knew him. I know of him only through others, and through having seen at least four different sittings for his photograph, and four of his written prescriptions.

I visited his grave twenty years ago, when the wire fence that surrounded the small cemetery was falling down but the grave was covered with flowers; it was All Souls' Day. When I visited his grave on All Souls' Day in 1950, I found the small cemetery of twenty-five graves surrounded by a substantial wire fence and the grave of Don Pedrito well cared for. It will not become a "lost grave."

Pedro Jaramillo very definitely belonged to the lower social class and his manner of living showed that he had no desire to live above that level. His large Mexican hat was the only pretentious article of his apparel. This was stolen after his death, as was a gold watch that had been given to him. He could have lived in a better house if he had cared to, but his home was that of the poorest Mexican—a hut made of logs, daubed with mud, and thatched, I am sure, with bear-grass, such as was often seen in those days—a *jacal!* He didn't wear the shop-made boots of the better class of ranch Mexicans, but rather the heavy, coarse shoes that are worn by the peons in Mexico when they do not wear *guaraches* (sandals). The different suits of clothes that he had his picture taken in were presents to him, I was told.

An old cowboy, Jim Walker, of Alice, Texas, who had seen Don Pedrito, and had secured prescriptions from him, said that he had the quick, running walk of the Mexican peon, the man who works on foot. This helps to bear out the report that he had been a shepherd in an earlier time of his life, and perhaps had worked at other daily labor.

A brother of mine, who in the 1890's rode the range of the locality where Don Pedrito lived, said that he saw him often. He pronounced him brusque. That meant, I am sure, that he would pass this young cowboy on the way without stopping for the usual exchange of the amenities customary in those days when one met another on the road. It might have been that Don Pedrito's singleness of purpose in his work would allow him little time for such irrelevancies. I am sure that my brother never saw him off his horse. When asked if he appeared skilled in horsemanship, his reply was an emphatic "No." Yet Don Pedrito did cover hundreds, thousands, of miles on horseback during the twenty-five years he went about his work.

Pedro Jaramillo believed in himself; he believed that God had selected him for a work, had bestowed a vocation on him. Surely he never wavered in that belief, or he could not have dedicated himself so completely to the work at which he labored for a full twenty-five years after coming to Texas from Mexico.

He claimed that faith was the power he worked through. And the Mexican people, naturally deeply religious and strong in faith, were his principal disciples. All who knew him are agreed that he was a good man, honest and sincere, one who did all that he could to relieve the suffering of his fellow men.

It is true that some of the stories that are told may have been somewhat exaggerated, but they were told in good faith, nevertheless. Among the comparatively few stories that I tell—for they could be collected, given the effort, by the hundreds—the one that could tax one's credulity the most is the one about the shepherd sleeping on the piece of canvas in the water. I make a point of taking no liberty with what is told to me, or I should at least have had him floating on a cowhide, which would have been more appropriate. This story was told to me by an old man who had walked nine miles to return fifty cents he had borrowed from me to buy some medicine for his boy who had been bitten by a rattlesnake. I didn't like to discredit the story of such an honest man, but I hesitated to include it; so I tested it by repeating it to different ones whom I had confidence in, and everyone assured me that Don Pedrito, through the power of God, could have accomplished this miracle. Therefore I gave it a place in my collection.

Then I thought of Elisha the man of God, of how he caused the ax head to "swim" in the River Jordan. So, if God had given Elisha a *don,* as the Mexicans call a supernatural gift, by which he made the ax head swim, could He not have given Don Pedrito the *don* that enabled him to make the piece of canvas, with the pillow on it, to say nothing of the shepherd on top of that, swim in Los Olmos Creek? That is the Mexican way of reasoning. "Con el poder de Dios," a Mexican will say, meaning that with God's power nothing is impossible.

SoLEDAD PÉREZ *was born and reared in El Paso, Texas. Her interest in folklore began early in life. In the summers she would spend three months on her grandparents' ranch near the pueblo of Carichic in Chihuahua, Mexico. It was the custom of the family to remain at the table and tell stories every night. All participated, but her grandmother had the largest store of folktales. Miss Pérez now teaches English at Texas Western College in El Paso.*

MEXICAN FOLKLORE
FROM AUSTIN, TEXAS

CONDITIONS OF COLLECTION

The material for this collection I obtained by visiting in the city market, drug stores, fruit stores, tortilla factories, churches, and homes of Mexican people of Austin, Texas, in the fall and spring of 1948 and 1949.

The tales and other folkloric material were not taken down on a wire recorder. Notes were made in longhand as the informants talked and the stories were written up as soon as possible after that. The bulk of the material was written in Spanish, and English translations were made later.

No informants were noted down for the proverbs and riddles since these were recorded as the opportunity offered itself. Anywhere and at any time that a proverb or saying was heard during the course of a conversation, a notation was made. In some instances, the recorder was not even a participant in the conversations. Many of the proverbs and sayings were noted as Mexican people talked while they gathered at street corners or rode buses. As literal a translation as possible has been given of the proverbs. Some of them, of course, have no great meaning in such a translation; so the sense is given in idiomatic English or in the equivalent English proverb, provided one exists. Since most of the riddles involve a play on Spanish words, it is impossible to put them into English and make the play apparent.

The nineteen informants who contributed the folktales, beliefs, and remedies were adults, with the exception of two girls who were eleven and twelve years old. Half of the informants were born in Mexico, the others in the United States. Eleven preferred to recount the stories in Spanish and three preferred English. The two girls (7 and 8) told their stories together. The informants were:

1. Mrs. Charles G. Balagia
2. Mrs. Cecilia G. Vda. de Hernández
3. Mrs. Barbara Salinas
4. Mrs. Marta Vidaurri
5. Mrs. Noemí Ortega
6. Miss Lily Hernández
7. Gloria Prado
8. Rachel Solíz
9. Roberto Galván
10. Pedro Rincón
11. Ezequiel Rodríguez
12. Abel Ortega
13. Rubén Ortega Sr.
14. Sabás López
15. Pedro Naranjo
16. Mrs. Máxima Ochoa
17. Mrs. Luisa Chávez
18. José Gonzáles
19. Mrs. Angela Murillo

For the sake of comparison I have made references to works by Stith Thompson, A. M. Espinosa, and Ralph S. Boggs. A number such as "N532" indicates a motif as classified in Thompson's *Motif-Index of Folk-Literature* (Helsinki, Finland; Bloomington, Indiana; 1932-36). "Type 333" is from Thompson's *Types of the Folk-Tale* (Helsinki, 1928), a translation and revision of Antti Aarne's earlier classification. "Espinosa 271" refers to a story of that number and the comparative notes on it in Espinosa's *Cuentos Populares Españoles* (Madrid, 1946-1947). "Boggs 2023" is a number in Boggs's *Index of Spanish Folktales* (Chicago, 1930).

THE WEEPING WOMAN

THE TALE of the Weeping Woman (La Llorona) is not new. It is essentially a Mexican tale that has existed since Aztec times. According to Thomas A. Janvier[1] and Luis González Obregón,[2] the tale is based on Aztec mythology.

Both Janvier and Obregón refer to Bernardino de Sahagún[3] to point out the connection existing between the Weeping Woman and the Aztec goddess named Civacoatl, Cihuacohuatl, or Tonantzin who appeared dressed in white and bearing a cradle on her shoulders as though she were carrying a child. The goddess mixed among the Aztec women and left the cradle abandoned. When the women looked into the cradle, they always found an arrowhead shaped like the Aztec sacrificial knife. At night the goddess went through the cities and towns shrieking and weeping and disappeared in the waters of lakes or rivers.

Later, the myth became merged with the story of real tragedy, usually a story involving a crime, such as infanticide. Vicente Riva Palacio and Juan de Dios Peza retell a 16th-century tale of Luisa, a beautiful peasant girl who fell in love with Don Muño Montes Claros and bore him three sons.[4] When Don Muño abandoned Luisa to marry a woman of his own class, Luisa murdered the children and then went through the streets shrieking and sobbing. Don Muño committed suicide.

Today, the tale of the Weeping Woman is current throughout Mexico. In the United States it is also known in Texas, California, Arizona, and possibly other states. Betty Leddy has listed forty-two versions in her study, "La Llorona in Southern Arizona," published in *Western Folklore*, VII (1948), 272-77. No similar study has been made for Texas or California.

The Weeping Woman is well known in Austin. Most of my informants had come from Mexico and had known it before they came here. In some instances the tale has become localized. The Weeping Woman is often said to be someone who lived in Austin many years ago; she killed her children, and now her spirit wanders about.

In Austin, La Llorona appears in many shapes and forms. Some informants contend that she is a woman with a seductive figure and a horse face. Others hold that she is a woman dressed in black, having long hair, shiny, tin-like fingernails, and a

[1]*Legends of the City of Mexico* (New York, 1910), pp. 134-138, 162-165.
[2]*Las Calles de México* (7th ed.; México, D. F., 1947), vol. I, pp. 37-40.
[3]*Historia de Nueva España* (México, D. F., 1890), vol. I, bk. I, pp. 32-33.
[4]*Tradiciones y Leyendas Méxicanas* (México, n.d.), pp. 127-149.

skeleton's face. A few believe that she is a vampire that sucks its victim's blood. The majority insist that she is a woman dressed in white, with long black hair, long fingernails, and the face of a bat. The Weeping Woman's failure to repent and confess her sins has become affixed to two of the stories.

An unlimited number of personalized stories can be built on "La Llorona." Not all of such stories that I have heard in Austin are included here.

THE WEEPING WOMAN (1)

A LONG time ago there was a woman who had two children. She did not love them; so she mistreated and neglected them. The children were always hungry and cold because their mother was too busy going to parties and dances to take care of them.

Finally one of the children died and later the other died too. The woman felt no remorse. She continued to lead a very gay life. When she died, she had not confessed her sins or repented of her ill-treatment of the children. Now she appears in the east and southeast parts of Austin grieving for her children. Her soul is doing penance for her sins.

(Informant 2. E411, V22.)

THE WEEPING WOMAN (2)

Do you know why La Llorona appears near the Colorado River? Well, La Llorona was a woman who lived here in Austin. She had two children, but she didn't love them. One day she took them to the river and drowned them. She never repented, and that is why she appears there and cries for her children.

My son, Rodolfo, was ten or eleven years old when he and some other boys decided to spend the night out near the river. They went in a little cart and took some blankets.

At night they spread the blankets out on the ground and went to sleep. He says that after midnight all of them woke up at the same time and saw a shadow flit across them. Then they heard the piercing wail of La Llorona. They got up and came home immediately. My son was very frightened when he got home.

(Informant 2.)

She had the face of a horse.

THE WEEPING WOMAN (3)

My BROTHER had a very good friend who was a shoemaker. The two were heavy drinkers, and they liked to go out together to eat and drink.

Well, one night my brother went to see his friend about twelve-thirty and prevailed on him to go out to drink with him.

Shortly after the two had started out for their favorite saloon, they noticed that a very attractive woman was walking just ahead of them. They decided to follow her. The two followed for a long time, but they couldn't catch up with her. When it seemed that they were coming up even with the woman, she suddenly seemed to get about half a block ahead of them. Finally, my brother and his friend decided to turn back, but as a parting gesture they said, "Good-by, my dear!"

At the same time that the two said, "Good-by, my dear!" the attractive woman whom they had followed turned around. She had the face of a horse, her fingernails were shiny and tin-like, and she gave a long, piercing cry. It was La Llorona.

My brother would have run, but his friend had fainted, and he had to revive him. The two reformed after that encounter with La Llorona.

(Informant 3.)

THE WEEPING WOMAN (4)

My FATHER was a missionary, and on one occasion he held a religious service in Atoyac, Michoacán. We lived in the neighboring town of Coyoacán, and after the service we left for home. It was rather late at night, but there was a full moon.

Some friends, my father and I were traveling along, carefree, when we heard a scream. The dog that was with us growled and tried to hide. We saw a shadow flit by, and a moment later we heard another scream in front of us. My hair stood on end. It was La Llorona.

(Informant 3.)

THE RETURN OF THE GARDENER

THE RETURN of the Gardener is similar, in some respects, to the tale of the Golden Arm, which is well known in the South. The approach of the light, the ghostlike noises, and the final death of the one guilty of theft or murder is the same in both stories; but this tale differs from that of the Golden Arm in that no theft of part of the corpse takes place. The gardener is murdered and a stew is made of his flesh. It is not specified that the entrails alone were used in the preparation of the stew, and it is not clear why the gardener insists on their return only.

This tale is usually narrated to children as a bedtime story. The narrator may draw out the approach of the light and the tinkling of the bell so long that the children fall asleep before the end of the tale.

THERE WAS once a poor married couple. The man was a gardener, and he had many friends whom he loved dearly. He suggested to his wife that they invite these friends to supper, but his wife refused because they had nothing to give them. But the gardener kept insisting, and the friends were invited.

The day of the supper came, and the gardener's wife had nothing to give the guests; so she killed the gardener and made a delicious stew.

Several weeks passed and then several months. The gardener's wife was beginning to forget that she had killed her husband, but one night she saw a light far off in the distance, and she heard the faintest tinkle of a bell that went, "Ting-a-ling, ting-a-ling!"

The second night the light seemed to be nearer, and the tinkle of the bell was more distinct. It went, "Ting-a-ling, ting-a-ling!"

The third night the light drew nearer, and the tinkling of the bell was more and more distinct. It went, "Ting-a-ling, ting-a-ling!"

The fourth night the light was just outside the window, and the bell went, "Ting-a-ling, ting-a-ling!"

The fifth night the light was in the house. The tinkling of the bell was very clear, but the woman also began to hear her husband's voice. It said, "I have come for my entrails!"

The sixth night the light came closer to the woman's bed, and the tinkling of the bell and her husband's voice were louder. The bell went, "Ting-a-ling, ting-a-ling!" Her husband's voice said, "I have come for my entrails!"

Then the seventh night it was next to her bed. Suddenly her husband's voice said, "I have caught you!" The poor woman screamed and died of fright.

(Informant 9. E235.4.)

THE FAT MAN

THE FAT MAN is a cumulative tale, a variety of the Troll Tale in which the giant devours men and animals. At last the troll is cut open and all are rescued alive.

The tale as narrated by my informants has been Americanized. The children are sent to the store to buy bread, butter, ham, and eggs.

ONCE UPON a time there lived a very happy family. The father, the mother, the son, the daughter, and the pet monkey lived happily in a little house.

One day, the mother said to the son, "Go to the store and buy bread, ham, butter, and eggs."

The little boy went to the store, but on the way he met a very big fat man. The man had a deep, hoarse voice. He asked the little boy, "Where are you going?"

The little boy answered, "I am going to the store."

The little boy went on to the store, but when he was going back home the big fat man met him and said, "Give me what you have!" The little boy gave him what he had bought, and the man ate everything at once. Then he took the little boy and ate him, too.

Since the little boy did not return home, the mother told the little girl, "Go and buy the bread, the ham, the butter, and the eggs."

The little girl went to the store, and she was returning home when the fat man met her. He said, "What do you have?"

The little girl answered, "I have bread, ham, butter, and eggs."

The fat man said, "Well, give them to me!" The little

girl gave them to the man, and he ate everything. Then he took the little girl and ate her up.

It grew dark, and the children did not return home; so the mother told the father, "Go and look for the children and buy the bread, the ham, the butter, and the eggs."

The father went to the store and bought all that his wife had told him to buy. He asked about the children and looked for them, but he could not find them. Tired and sad, the father started back home, but on the way the fat man came out and said, "Who are you and what do you have in that basket?"

The father of the children answered, "I am a poor man who is looking for his children. I have bread, ham, butter, and eggs in this basket."

The fat man said, "Give me what you have. I ate the children, and I shall eat you, too!" He took the basket and ate everything. Then he ate the father.

The mother was very tired of waiting; so she went to the store and to look for her husband and children. She looked and looked, but she found nothing. Finally, the mother started back home, but on the way the fat man met her. He said, "Who are you and what do you have?"

The mother said, "I am a poor woman looking for her husband and children. I have bread, ham, butter, and eggs in my basket."

The fat man said, "Give me everything. I ate your husband and children, and I shall eat you, too." Then he ate everything and the mother too.

Only the pet monkey was left at home, and when he saw that no one returned, he started out in search of the father and the family. The monkey looked and looked, and finally he met the fat man. The monkey asked him, "Have you seen a man, a woman, and some children?"

The fat man said, "Yes, I ate them, and I shall eat you too!"

The fat man ate the monkey, but the monkey had a big knife. When he reached the fat man's stomach, he found the father, the mother, and the children. The monkey gave the knife to the father, and he cut open the fat man's stomach. All were freed. The fat man died, and the family lived happily ever after.

(Informants 7 and 8. Types 333, 2028.)

THE WANDERING PRINCE

THE TALE of the Wandering Prince is related to the tale of the Wandering Jew, though the prince is not condemned to wander as a punishment. When he asked for unending life, he did not foresee how lonely he would be as he lost his friends to death. The informant did not know the story of the Wandering Jew. The prince is also somewhat like Tithonus, who wished for eternal life but forgot to wish for eternal youth.

ONCE UPON a time there was a prince who was very handsome and rich, but he was very sad. One day the princess asked him, "Why are you so sad?"

He answered, "I am sad because I see that everything dies and I do not want to die. I want to be immortal."

"But you cannot be immortal," the princess said. "Besides, there are many beautiful things in this world such as the trees, the flowers, the sky, love, hope, faith, and much more."

But the prince did not heed the princess. He became sadder and sadder. Finally he decided to go see a hermit who lived in a cave. He went to the cave and the hermit came out and said, "What do you want with me, Prince? You have everything your heart desires."

The prince said, "Yes, I have everything my heart desires, but I see that everything dies and that saddens me. I want to be immortal, and I want you to make me immortal."

The hermit asked him, "Have you thought about it seriously? Go back home for a week, and if at the end of that time you still want to be immortal, come back to me."

The week passed, and the prince returned to the hermit's cave. He knocked at the door of the cave, but instead of the hermit a woman with a veiled face came out. She asked the prince what he wanted, and he repeated his wish that he be given immortality. The woman fascinated the prince, and finally he asked, "Why do you keep your face veiled? Is it that you are so beautiful that one may not gaze on your face?"

The woman said, "No, I am not beautiful. I am very ugly,

but sometime you will love me and call me to come to you."

This made the prince very curious to find out who the woman was. He insisted so much that she consented to raise her veil. When she did so, the prince screamed and said, "You are Death! Go away! I will never love you or call you!"

The woman disappeared, and the hermit came out. He asked the prince, "Are you certain that you want to be immortal?"

The prince said, "Yes, I am more certain of it than ever."

Then the hermit gave the prince some magic potions. A short time passed, and suddenly the prince jumped up and began to shout, "I am immortal! I am immortal!"

Many years passed, and the prince went from kingdom to kingdom. Wherever a war was being fought, the prince could be found. He was an excellent soldier, and since nothing hurt him, he fought with great valor; but time passed, and the prince became bored with everything. One day after a battle in which some of his dearest friends had fallen, the prince looked about and said bitterly, "Oh, Death! I never thought that I would love you, but I have come to love you. Come to my side that I may die."

Death did not come. The prince was immortal, and today he still wanders over the face of the earth.

(Informant 4. Type 754***. Q502.1, M416.2.)

RATONCITO PÉREZ

THIS TALE of the little ant's courtship and marriage is widespread in Spain and Spanish America. With its succession of animal suitors and the repetition of questions and answers, it is much liked by children. Forty-six folk versions have been recorded, and writers of children's books have often retold "La Hormiguita," as it is usually called. The tale is kin to the English song of the frog who married a mouse.

ONCE there was an ant. Like other ants she was very hardworking.

One day the ant found a real, and she said to herself, "What shall I buy? If I buy candy, I will eat it. If I buy a broom, it will wear out."

Finally she decided to buy a dress, some little boots, and a ribbon for her hair. So she did. Then she put on the dress,

He said to the little ant, "My, you are beautiful,
little ant! Don't you want to marry me?"

the little boots, and the ribbon and sat out in front of her house.

Soon a cat went by and said, "My, you are beautiful, little ant! Don't you want to marry me?"

The little ant replied, "How will you speak to me after we are married?"

"I will say mew, mew," answered the cat.

"No, you frighten me," said the little ant.

In a little while a dog went by and said, "My, you are beautiful, little ant! Don't you want to marry me?"

The little ant asked, "How will you speak to me after we are married?"

"I will say bowwow, bowwow," answered the dog.

"No, you frighten me," said the little ant.

A bull came by and said, "My, you are beautiful, little ant! Don't you want to marry me?"

The little ant answered, "How will you speak to me after we are married?"

"I will say moo, moo," answered the bull.

"No, you frighten me," said the little ant.

A lamb came by and said, "My, you are beautiful, little ant! Don't you want to marry me?"

The little ant answered, "How will you speak to me after we are married?"

"I will say baa, baa," said the lamb.

"No, you frighten me," said the little ant.

Finally Ratoncito Pérez passed by. Ratoncito Pérez was very clean and well combed.

He said to the little ant, "My, you are beautiful, little ant! Don't you want to marry me?"

The little ant answered, "How will you speak to me after we are married?"

Ratoncito Pérez had a very sweet voice.

"I will say ee, ee, ee."

"I like that! You shall be my husband, Ratoncito Pérez," said the little ant. She was very happy.

The little ant and Ratoncito Pérez lived happily for a long time.

One day when the little ant went out, she told Ratoncito Pérez, "Take care of the soup until I come back."

Ratoncito Pérez peered down into the soup and fell in.

When the little ant returned she found Ratoncito Pérez dead. All the little animals came and tried to comfort her, but they could not. The little ant would not be comforted. Even to this day she grieves and mourns for Ratoncito Pérez and his sweet voice.

(Informants 7 and 8. Espinosa 271-274; Boggs 2023.)

THE REAL

THIS IS a formula tale of how an old woman finds a real, buys a ladder, and attempts, along with certain animals, to climb to Heaven. It does not belong to a type established by students of the folktale, thought it has a pattern similar to that of Ratoncito Pérez, which has been related above. The Tower of Babel motif may be present, but it is not stressed. As in Ratoncito Pérez, the number of animals in The Real may be varied.

ONCE UPON a time, there was a little old lady. She was very hard-working, and was always sweeping the courtyard of her home.

One day the little old lady found a real. She said, "What shall I buy with the real? If I buy corn, it will not last. If I buy a broom, it will wear out." The little old lady thought for a long time, and finally she decided. She said, "I am going to buy a ladder to climb to heaven." The little old lady bought a ladder, and she had it placed in the courtyard of her home.

The little old lady was climbing the ladder when a cat passed by. He asked her, "What are you doing, little old lady?"

The little old lady answered, "I am going to climb to Heaven."

The cat said, "Won't you let me climb too?"

The little old lady said, "All right, you may climb."

Then a dog passed by, and he asked the cat, "What are you doing, little cat?"

The cat answered, "The little old lady bought a ladder, and we are going to climb to Heaven."

The dog said, "Won't you let me climb too?"

The cat said, "All right, you may climb."

Then a cow passed by, and she asked the dog, "What are you doing, little dog?"

The dog answered, "The little old lady bought a ladder, and we are going to climb to Heaven."

The cow said, "Won't you let me climb too?"

The dog said, "All right, you may climb."

Then a donkey passed by, and he asked the cow, "What are you doing, little cow?"

The cow answered, "The little old lady bought a ladder, and we are going to climb to Heaven."

The donkey said, "Won't you let me climb too?"

The cow said, "All right, you may climb."

Then a horse passed by, and he asked the donkey, "What are you doing, little donkey?"

The donkey answered, "The little old lady bought a ladder, and we are going to climb to Heaven."

The horse said, "Won't you let me climb too?"

The donkey said, "All right, you may climb."

Then a rooster passed by, and he asked the horse, "What are you doing, little horse?"

The horse answered, "The little old lady bought a ladder, and we are going to climb to Heaven."

The rooster said, "Won't you let me climb too?"

The horse said, "All right, you may climb."

Then a lion passed by, and he asked the rooster, "What are you doing, little rooster?"

The rooster answered, "The little old lady bought a ladder, and we are going to climb to Heaven."

The lion said, "Won't you let me climb too?"

The rooster said, "All right, you may climb."

Then a tiger passed by, and he asked the lion, "What are you doing, little lion?"

The lion answered, "The little old lady bought a ladder, and we are going to climb to Heaven."

The tiger said, "Won't you let me climb too?"

The lion said, "All right, you may climb."

Finally, an elephant passed by, and he asked the tiger, "What are you doing, little tiger?"

The tiger answered, "The little old lady bought a ladder, and we are going to climb to Heaven."

The elephant said, "Won't you let me climb too?"

The tiger said, "All right, you may climb."

The little old lady and the animals were climbing higher and higher. Suddenly, the ladder broke, and all fell to the earth. The little old lady was left without a real, without a ladder, and without having climbed to Heaven.

(Informants 7 and 8. Boggs 2023. F52, F772.1, C771.1.)

TALES OF THE DEVIL

A POPULAR belief among the Mexicans of Austin is that the Devil may assume any form he chooses and make himself visible to human beings to punish disobedience, vice, and sinful acts. In the tales narrated by my informants, the Devil assumes the form of a human, a ball of fire, a dog, and a sow.

THE STRANGER

THE DEVIL appears very frequently at dances that last many hours. One time he appeared all dressed up in formal clothes. As soon as he came in, all the ladies cast admiring glances at him. But he disregarded them and went to dance with a very beautiful woman who attended every dance and usually stayed out very late. They danced six or seven pieces, and everyone was filled with admiration because he danced like a professional. After he finished dancing the seventh piece, he turned and said, "This is the way to dance, and don't be fools!"

But a woman had been watching him very closely, and she said, "Yes, you dance very well, but what is wrong with your feet? God protect us! You aren't the Devil, are you?"

When he heard this, the Devil disappeared immediately in a sulphurous cloud of smoke. The girl with whom he had been dancing was found unconscious with her face all scratched up.

(Informant 9. G303.3.1.2.)

LIDIA AND THE DEVIL

THERE WAS a girl, Lidia, who was very beautiful but very disobedient. She wanted to go to a dance, but her mother said that she couldn't go. Lidia did not obey her mother.

When Lidia was at the dance, a very handsome man walked in. Everyone looked at him. Lidia looked at him too, and wished that he would dance with her, but there were many other beautiful girls; so she thought that he would not. Lidia was surprised when he came and invited her to dance. They danced together all night, and when Lidia went home, he accompanied her.

When Lidia and the man arrived at her house, she noticed that there was something strange about him. He seemed to have changed. His eyes seemed to glow in the darkness, and he limped somewhat. Lidia felt great fear. She crossed herself and said, "Jesus, Mary, and Joseph!" She tried to scream, but she fainted. When Lidia regained consciousness, her mother had placed her on a bed and was weeping. Lidia asked, "Where is the man who accompanied me home?"

Her mother answered, "It was the Devil. Your face is all scratched."

(Informant 2. G303.3.1.)

MATASIETE

You know Madero and his cabinet and ministers used to come to Monclova, Coahuila. When they came, they had a big celebration. Madero always stayed at the Hotel de los Chinos (Hotel of the Chinese). It was called that way because it was owned and run by Chinese.

Well, one of the times when Madero came, we went to sing to him, and while we were there a lot of shooting started. Madero had his paymaster with him, and "Matasiete" (Killer of Seven) and his band had tried to rob the paymaster.

During the shooting, one of my aunts was caught right in the middle of it, and—would you believe it?—all the bullets went right between her legs and didn't hurt her.

After the shooting was over, Matasiete was left lying on the ground. They wouldn't let the people gather around him, and they put ice around him because they couldn't give him medical aid or anything until the law took note of the happenings. We passed near Matasiete and all of his stomach was open, but he wasn't dead. He stayed there all that afternoon and night. The next day he died at ten o'clock in the morning.

Just as soon as Matasiete died the wind started blowing. That is unusual in Monclova. Well, the wind kept blowing harder and harder. Finally some men were told to bury Matasiete. They called a priest to come and officiate, but he refused. The men brought a cart and put the dead man in, but the horses refused to move. They tried everything, but still the horses would not move. The men went to the priest again and asked him to help them bury Matasiete. They compromised, and he agreed to go if another priest went along. The two priests went. They had to sprinkle holy water and take the horses' bridles to lead them all the way to the outskirts of the city. It was the only way they could get the horses to move.

Matasiete was buried, and the next day when curious people went to look at the grave they found imprints of the Devil's claws on some boulders nearby.

Matasiete was not a human being but the Devil.

(Informant 1. G303.3.1, E411.0.3.)

THE BALL OF FIRE

MANY TIMES I had heard people say that the Devil appears to men and women. I didn't believe it, but this is what happened at the Hacienda de los Albarcones in Nuevo León, Mexico.

There were two huge basins of water of about a mile in circumference where the cattle were watered, especially in times of drought. High levees surrounded these basins, and our house and that of a friend, Julio, stood below one of them.

This happened on Saturday of Holy Week. On Holy Week it was customary to fly kites, and there were many other amusements.

On Saturday it was customary for the Judas to be taken about the streets on a donkey or a cart. The men in charge of the Judas stopped at each house and asked for a gift for the Judas. Each person gave whatever he was able to. According to the gift received, the men recited a little verse of thanks. In this way, the Judas was paraded all over the village, and at twelve o'clock it was taken in procession to a certain place chosen beforehand. There, the young boys and others threw stones and poked the Judas with sticks. Finally they lighted a gunpowder charge placed in the Judas, and it exploded.

All this took place, and in the afternoon we flew kites. We had such a good time flying the kites that it was dark before we started home. It was about nine o'clock when one of the boys, Julio, left. He walked along the edge of the levee, which was quite high.

As Julio walked along, he noticed that at the exact place where the Judas had been burned a sudden flame of fire shot up. He kept on walking, but on turning back to see the place where the flame had appeared, he saw a ball of fire. The ball started rolling up to the levee's edge, and soon it was rolling after Julio. It was not more than twenty-five yards away from him; so he began to run as fast as he could. He was almost home. Julio ran down the embankment with the ball of fire close behind him. Fortunately, a light was burning in his home, and as Julio reached the door he fell and lost consciousness. He remained unconscious for twenty-four hours. All the people said that it was the Devil chasing him and that the only thing that saved Julio was the light burning in the window. Light is a protection against the Devil and evil spirits.

(Informant 10.)

THE SPOTTED POOCH

IN AUSTIN, many Mexican people have been attracted by a little dog. He is just a little spotted pooch, black and white or brown and white. He appears on the eastern streets of the city, especially on East Sixth Street. The little dog is such an unusual pooch that people seeing him wish to have him. When they try to catch him, he is very elusive. He follows a set route, and when he reaches a certain corner, he disappears. Some contend that he is the Devil, and others that there is buried treasure at the exact location where he disappears.

(Informant 15. G303.3.3.1.)

THE SOW IN THE PLAZA

MY BROTHER liked liquor very much. One night in Guadalajara, Jalisco, at the Plaza of the Hospicio, he and some friends saw a sow with her little pigs. They thought that it was unusual for a sow and her pigs to be in the Plaza at that time of the night, so they followed her for a while. Suddenly, she disappeared into a tiny hole. It was the Devil.

(Informant 15. G303.3.3.4.)

GHOST TALES

THE MEXICANS have many beliefs concerning death because they stand in great awe and reverence of it. One of these beliefs is that one who dies after receiving all the spiritual aids of the church will go either to Purgatory to be cleansed of his sins or to Heaven immediately. But if one dies without confessing one's sins or receiving the last sacred rites of the church, his soul will go to Purgatory or to Hell. Yet these dead may, on occasion, make friendly or unfriendly returns to earth. Other souls are bound to the earth and cannot rest until their bonds are loosened, because they have died leaving unfulfilled vows, unpaid debts or promises, unrevealed secrets, or other ties. These souls appear most frequently seeking mortal aid to loosen the bonds so that they may rest. Some appear to predict disaster or death while others may appear to punish wrongs. Sometimes the apparition is accompanied by ghostlike noises. Frequently the ghosts are heard without being seen.

THE COLD, CLAMMY HAND

WE USED to live in a two-story house on First Street, and my father lived with us. After putting the children to bed, I always went upstairs to see if they were covered.

One night I had gone up to see them, and on the way downstairs I suddenly felt a chill as if someone with a very cold and clammy hand had touched the nape of my neck. I turned around but saw nothing. At the foot of the stairs I had a sofa, and I saw that a man was sitting there. It was dark and I thought it was Daddy; so I said, "Daddy, are you home?" There was no answer. I reached the bottom of the stairs and flicked on the light, but there was no one sitting on the sofa.

About three weeks later, Daddy came home very sick. We put him to bed and took good care of him. On the night of the sixteenth of September he asked me, "Why don't you go to the celebration? You like those things!"

"Well," I replied, "when you feel better, both of us can go out and celebrate. What do you say?"

I came downstairs after that, and as I came down I again felt the cold, clammy hand brush the nape of my neck. I stayed in the living room and listened to the music, but I couldn't shake off an uneasy feeling.

Next morning, I washed Daddy up and asked him what he wanted for breakfast. He said, "Oh, anything you bring me will be all right."

I went downstairs, and I had just put a pot of water on to boil when my brother came in. He said, "I meant to come in last night, but we went to the celebration, and it was too late when we got home. How is Dad?"

I told him that Dad was much better and asked that he prop him up with pillows while I finished fixing his breakfast. As I started back to the kitchen, I felt the same cold chill that I had experienced before.

My brother had gone upstairs, and suddenly I heard him scream as loud as you please. I tried to run up the stairs but I fell down. I still don't know how I got up there, but when I walked into Dad's room, my brother said, "What do you mean that Dad is better? He is dead!"

Dad was dead exactly a month after I had felt the clammy hand and seen the ghost.

(Informant 1. E421.1.1, E545.2.)

LA ESPERANZA

A YOUNG man and a young woman met, fell in love, and decided to marry. The young man was to inherit an hacienda from his father, but the young man did not want it because it was haunted.

The day of the wedding, the bridegroom's father gave the hacienda to his son, but his son said that he did not want it.

The young wife wanted it very much, and she asked her father-in-law to go ahead and give it to them. The father-in-law did so. The young man refused to go there to live, but the girl insisted so much that the young husband finally consented.

On their way to the hacienda, the husband told his wife that when he was small there was a bedroom at the hacienda where a hand appeared before a mirror. The beautiful hand was seen as it passed across the mirror, and then a sigh was heard. The young wife laughed and said that she did not believe such things. She wanted to spend a few days in that bedroom to see if she could hear or see anything herself.

The couple arrived at the hacienda, and at nightfall it began to rain very hard. They retired to the bedroom. Suddenly they saw a beautiful hand pass in front of the mirror. Then they heard a sigh, long and full of sadness. The young wife was greatly surprised, but she told her husband, "I am going to discover what is going on."

She and her husband examined the room. Behind the full-length mirror they found a door; with great difficulty they opened it and discovered a small room. There on a table was a jewel box and a letter which read thus:

"These jewels must be given to the first child who is born in this hacienda. I was a married woman and the owner of this hacienda. We were a very happy couple until my husband was killed. The baby which I was expecting was never born. Now just before I die I want to ask of anyone who finds this letter that if the first child born in the hacienda be a girl she be named Esperanza (Hope). As long as this letter and its orders are not fulfilled, my spirit will wander over the hacienda."

The young couple want on living at the hacienda. Their first child was a little girl whom they named Esperanza and to whom they gave the jewels. The hand never appeared again, and they all lived happily ever after. The hacienda was always known by the name of La Esperanza.

(Informant 4. 'E451.3.)

A VISIT WITH THE DEAD

THERE were two intimate men friends, Manny and Zeke.

Manny was drafted, and eventually he was sent overseas. Zeke was in ill health and remained at home in Austin. When Manny came home after being discharged, the first thing he did was to go and see his good friend Zeke. He knocked at the door and Zeke came out. They were very happy to see each other. They shook hands, slapped each other on the back, and then went into the house and chatted for about an hour and a half. Then Manny said that he had to go.

As Manny got up to leave, he noticed that many people were coming up the walk to the house. He went out to meet them, and the first one he met was Zeke's mother. She looked at him very strangely and said, "Well, what are you doing here?"

"I just got back," Manny replied, "and I had to come and see Zeke right away. He looks grand."

"Did you say that you saw Zeke?" the mother asked.

Manny said, "Certainly, we have been talking for over an hour!"

The woman began to cry.

"It couldn't be Zeke," she said, "because we buried him about half an hour ago. You have been talking with his spirit. He loved you so much that he had to come back and talk to you!"

(Informant 13. E300.)

THE MIDNIGHT CALL

MY GRANDMOTHER'S eldest son was named Ezequiel. Since he was the eldest, he was petted and allowed to do as he pleased. Once Ezequiel came to San Antonio and lost a fortune in gambling. Then he became very ill, but he would not go home because he was afraid of his mother and ashamed of having lost his money in gambling.

One night while Ezequiel was still very ill, he fell asleep, and he heard his mother's voice distinctly calling, "Ezequiel, Ezequiel, Ezequiel!"

He woke up and was startled to see a tall, dark figure standing at the foot of the bed.

As soon as Ezequiel was able to travel, he went home and told his mother about it.

"Yes," she said, "I knew something was wrong. When you didn't come home and we couldn't find you, I was desperate. I got up very late at night and prayed for you. Then I went outside and called your name three times. You heard my voice, and the person whom you saw was probably my mother. Now that you are back you are forgiven."

(Informant 1. E300.)

INDIAN RENDEZVOUS

ON FOGGY or rainy nights we used to hear much noise at 804 Red River Street when we were going to bed. We could hear footsteps as of Indians and saw shadowy forms. Many times the noise woke me up, and I could hear, "Bam, bam, bam." This continued all night long. I would pray, but the noise continued.

At other times it seemed as if a very heavy weight settled on Esther and me. We would get up and turn on the light, but there was nothing. As soon as we put out the light, the noise would start again.

One day while talking to an old American man, I was told that formerly there was an entrance to a cave where the house now stands. In this cave the Indians hid treasure and kept their horses after coming back from a raid. The entrance to the cave disappeared. It is not known whether the Indians sealed it up or whether a landslide or something like that covered it up. Anyway, it has never been found.

(Informant 2. E402.)

A DEAD MAN SPEAKS

MY COUSINS Andrés, Francisco, and Santiago had wanted to come to the United States for a long time. They were coming to see us, but they got on the wrong train, and instead of coming to Austin they went to Oklahoma. While there, they worked as cowboys.

Once while the three were out on the range, one of their fellow cowboys became ill. They took the cowboy to the nearest house, which was a two-room abandoned shack. The cowboy died, and the others put his body on some planks in one of the rooms and placed a candle at the head of the body and another at the foot.

Then one of the cowboys suggested a game of cards to while away the time. My cousin Francisco objected. He said, "There's a dead man in the next room. We can't be disrespectful."

The others refused to hear. They began to play cards and drink whisky. One of the candles began to burn very low, and they had no other, so Andrés told Francisco, "Go into the other room and get one of the candles."

Francisco went into the room where the dead man lay. As he clutched the candle, the dead man raised himself up slightly. Francisco tripped, threw down the candle, and fell against the planks. The candle at the head of the body blew out and the planks flew up into the air. As they did so the dead man was thrown forward on Francisco. His elbows pricked Francisco and he heard a shrill voice say, "You must respect dead men."

At this, Francisco screamed, "Help, the dead man is killing me!"

When the cowboys heard this, they ran out of the shack. Andrés was the first to recover, and he went back to see what had happened to Francisco. Francisco had fainted. The cowboys revived him, but they didn't go back to the cards and whisky. They never again played or drank when they were around a dead man.

(Informant 1. E235.)

THE GERMAN GIRL

WHEN MY father and mother first came to Texas they were looking for a small ranch or farm. They went to see one between Hallettsville and Waelder.

On their arrival at the farm the owner took them to an old abandoned house and told them that they could spend the night there. The only thing inside was a mattress made out of cornshucks, on which my parents made their bed and went to sleep.

At about one o'clock in the morning, my mother woke up. She could hear a woman talking and screaming. She woke my father up and both of them listened, but they couldn't understand the woman's language. They knew it was not English, French, or Spanish, because my mother could have recognized these. The screaming and the talking seemed to come from a cave right under the house. Father got up and looked around, but he could not find a thing. The screaming and talking continued all night.

The next day my father told the owner what had happened and expressed no desire to buy the farm.

"Well," said the man, "I have been told that a German girl was thrown into a well that is under the house. She was thrown in alive and allowed to die there, but I think that if you pull up the boards and fill the well with dirt the noise would disappear."

My father and mother didn't want to stay there and left right away.

(Informant 1. E402.)

TALES OF BURIED TREASURE

BURIED TREASURE tales are similar to ghost tales in many respects. Men who have hidden money and died without disclosing its whereabouts, so the belief goes, cannot rest in peace until the treasure has been found. They appear as ghosts to indicate the location of the treasure. Others guard it.

All of these tales in this book deal with treasure buried by men. In most instances the presence of the buried treasure is made known by the appearance of lights, fires, or strange animals or by ghostlike noises such as the tramping of horses' hoofs. In others, men know of the location of the treasure because they helped to bury it.

The unearthing of the buried treasure is not always successfully carried out.

TREASURE AT THE HACIENDA DE LOS ALBARCONES

IT IS BELIEVED that the Hacienda of Albarcones in Nuevo León, Coahuila, was founded in 1600 by the Count of Jaral. My parents and grandparents, as well as I can remember, had lived and worked there in the Hacienda for many years.

Now the Hacienda is almost in ruins, but when I lived there, many houses and the church were still standing. Many people said that fires and flitting shadows could be seen in the church. Many heard sounds as of an earthquake at certain hours and certain days of the week. Usually these noises were heard twice a week at about two or three o'clock in the afternoon.

Well, in 1915, a young man, a descendant of the Count of Jaral, came to the Hacienda with an escort of soldiers and permission of the government to look for buried treasure in the church. He spoke with some of us and told us that he wanted us to work for him.

We went to the church. The young man brought a machine that looked like a phonograph. It was a German invention and had electric wire attachments. He placed this instrument upon a tripod and operated it with electricity. If the wires vibrated, they indicated that there was a magnet of some sort. He placed the instrument with the wires extending out to the four compass points. As soon as he did this one of the antennae began to vibrate. Only this antenna pointing to the north vibrated. Then he moved the machine around, and the antenna extending toward the north always vibrated when it was directly in front of the main altar of the church.

After the young man had marked the location, he ordered us to make an excavation. When we reached a depth of about six feet in the excavation, which was to be eight feet square, we were able to uncover something, and the young man said, "If any of you have avaricious thoughts or ideas, you had better get out."

No one said anything. After reaching a certain depth, we began to hear a hollow sound, and we were ordered to get out of the excavation. The young man then gave us a drink of liquor, saying, "Where money is buried, there is usually a fetid and poisonous gas that can kill a person."

After taking the liquor and covering our noses with handkerchiefs, we went down into the excavation with crowbars because the covering of the vault seemed to be made of cement. After uncovering a vault measuring approximately eight feet long by four feet wide, we found coal. We went ahead and pierced the vault with our crowbars, and the mortar broke right away. There was such a sudden rush of foul-smelling air that the coal was whipped up into a sort of whirlwind. After this we took away about a foot of coal that lay under the mortar. It was then that I saw what appeared to be two little lamps in one of the corners of the vault. They weren't lamps. They were two huge diamond rings, and from what I know now they must have been very valuable because they were huge. In another corner of the vault we found another ring. This one was red and shone so brilliantly that it seemed to burn. Then we found the remains of two skeletons. The remains of one were in the north corner of the vault, and the remains of the other were in the east corner. The young man was at a loss to explain the presence of the skeletons, but I believe that they must have been a husband and his wife. What astonished us was that the jewels were placed in two corners and the remains of the skeletons in the other two corners. The bones were all carefully piled together. The skull, arm bones, and all the other bones were carefully arranged in the form of the cross. They were so carefully placed together that it seemed as if some one had taken great pains to place them just so. The bones of the legs and arms of the skeleton in the north corner were very large, and those of the east corner were smaller, but both were arranged in the same manner. The gold of the jewels appeared shiny as if it were new, and the stones shone so brilliantly that they appeared to be flames.

After we took out all the jewels and the skeletons, we continued digging. There was another layer of mortar, and underneath lay the treasure. Under the layer of mortar were two copper kettles. One of them contained coins of two kinds of gold, yellow and red. The coins were square and as large as Mexican pesos. They looked as if they had just been minted. The other kettle contained silver coins. According to my estimate, there must have been about six thousand pesos in gold, and I don't know how much in silver.

The young man paid us and left for Mexico City. The sounds and the flitting shadows disappeared.

(Informant 10. E402, E283.)

HORSES' HOOFBEATS

MY GRANDFATHER used to tell us about a fire that he and some friends saw in Mexico. They saw it several times, so they decided to dig in search of buried treasure. They began to dig, and when it seemed that they had struck metal, they suddenly heard the tramping of horses' hoofs. They covered up the hole hurriedly and hid, but nothing happened. Again the men began to dig, but when they reached the same spot, the tramping of horses' hoofs was heard again. They decided to continue digging, but the noise of the horses' hoofs became so loud that they became very much afraid and covered up the hole. They never tried to dig again, and undoubtedly the treasure is still there.

(Informant 5. E402.)

THE SMUGGLERS' TREASURE

AN OLD MAN tells me that he lived in Matamoros around 1886. He was one of the smugglers who devoted themselves to amassing booty and transporting it into the interior of the republic.

At one time the band of smugglers had taken a large shipment of merchandise and money out of Matamoros. They had about 25,000 pesos. There were about thirty-five in their party, and they were well on their way to the interior when they were set upon by federal soldiers. Seeing that they were surrounded, the chief of the smugglers ordered his men to make a hole and bury the money in order to lighten their load so that each one could escape more easily.

The smugglers dug the hole only about four feet deep because they didn't have any more time, and they buried the money. When it was in the hole, the captain ordered them to mount their horses and pass by, making as much noise as possible with chains, spurs, and anything else. They did this before they began to cover the money. Afterwards, they covered it up while those on horseback continued to make noise. Finally they passed over the covered hole on their horses running at full speed. The captain told them when they had finished that they had had the pleasure of seeing and burying the money, but they no longer had any right to a single cent.

They were kept surrounded for eight days. During that time, they heard ghostlike noises at the exact spot where the treasure had been buried. At first they were frightened, thinking that the federal troops had caught them. Finally all escaped.

Years later the man and his son searched for the buried treasure, but they were unable to find it, although the man said that he knew the region and the place where the treasure was hidden as well as his hands.

(Informant 10.   N511.1.)

A STRANGE ANIMAL

A MAN and his family lived on a little ranch near Monclova, Coahuila. The man owned a saloon and a billiard parlor in town, so he frequently came home late at night. A big prickly pear tree grew near the house, and on several occasions as the man came by the prickly pear, an animal resembling a bear appeared. The man followed it, but it would disappear. He told his wife about it, and she suggested that they dig at the spot where the animal disappeared, but he was afraid that the animal might be the Devil.

Later the family sold the ranch, and the people who bought it knocked down the prickly pear tree. While plowing over the spot where the prickly pear had stood, they accidentally uncovered a box of money.

(Informant 2.   E520, B576.2.)

A WHITE LIGHT

AFTER I was married in Estancias, Coahuila, we lived near my father-in-law. My husband had a saloon and a billiard parlor, so he came home rather late. Well, his father died, and his mother went to live with her sister. She left the house entrusted to us. Since it was abandoned, it soon started falling down. The roof and part of a wall of one of the rooms that led into the kitchen collapsed.

One dark and rainy night my husband was coming home, and as he passed by the house he saw a white ray of light on the wall of the room where the roof and part of the wall had fallen. He came home, told me about it, and returned to the house with a pick and crowbar. He marked the place where the light shone, and on the following day he went and dug. He found nothing.

The people who lived around heard about it, but they said nothing. One day when I went to the house, I found that someone had just dug a hole in the floor of the chimney in the kitchen. It was apparent that the digger had taken out an *olla* (pot) because the shape and form of it had remained imprinted on the soil. I went to tell my husband about it, and when we returned all signs of the digging had disappeared. There was not the slightest trace that anyone had dug there. I am sure that I even saw a shovel on top of the heap of dirt. We were never able to find out what had happened, and we never discovered anything.

(Informant 2. N532.)

THE STAGECOACH

WHEN WE lived near Reforma, Coahuila, we were out one day, and we saw a stagecoach coming along the road. It was coming very fast and making a great deal of noise. It seemed to be white, and it had three teams of mules. We ran and told my mother, "Mother, company is coming."

My mother came out and saw the stagecoach coming. She went back into the house and hurriedly tried to tidy up the parlor. Then she came out again. We were all watching the stagecoach as it came nearer and nearer. Suddenly when it reached a place where two palms stand by the roadside, it disappeared. We were shocked to see this and entered the house trembling. When my father came home and we told him about it, we were still trembling with fear. He wouldn't believe our story.

A short time later we moved to Reforma, and a wealthy rancher bought our little ranch. It was said that he had heard about our experience and wanted to look for buried money. A stagecoach, carrying passengers and a great amount of money, had been held up at that spot. The passengers were killed, and the money was buried there when federal troops came up on the bandits.

Some people say that the rancher found the money, but we know that he didn't. It's probably still buried there. The next time a person sees that stagecoach, he should mark the place where it disappears and dig.

(Informant 2. E535.)

SAINTS' MIRACLES

IN THE acceptance of their religious faith, few people are as devout and sincere as the Mexicans. Firm believers in the doctrine that the good and the just will be rewarded and the evil and the unjust will be punished, they associate any unusual occurrence or phenomenon with the saints and the teachings of the Holy Church.

Of the many accounts of saints' miracles that I have heard in Austin, only a few are recorded here. One is illustrative of the latest miracles associated with the image of "El Niño Perdido" at Lacoste in Medina County, Texas; and two are of a humorous and paradoxical nature. (On saints' miracles in general cf. V220 in Thompson's *Motif-Index*.)

INNOCENCE PROVED

DURING the revolution, the rebels in Zacatecas arrested and tried those who favored the federal government. On one occasion they arrested a young man and sentenced him to be shot. He was a devout follower of Saint Joseph, and he maintained that he was innocent. He said that as a proof of his innocence it would rain in the afternoon on the day of his death. The rebels shot him one morning, and that afternoon it rained. The people said that Saint Joseph had proved the young man's innocence, and now they consider him a saint too.

(Informant 11. D2140.1.)

THE SAINT WHO DISAPPEARED

IN MY home town it rains very little. Many years ago there was a great drought; it didn't rain for three years. The priest met with the inhabitants of the town and took out San Lorenzo in his glass shrine, and they had a procession. They took the image to the outskirts of the town and left it there. San Lorenzo was to remain there until it rained. When the people returned a few days later to pray, they found that the saint's shrine was empty. The belief exists that the saint left the shrine through one of its sides. The people now speak of this saint as "El Santo Desaparecido."

(Informant 11. D2140.1.)

"EL NIÑO PERDIDO"

THERE IS an image in Lacoste, Medina County, Texas, named "El Niño Perdido." The people have given the saint this name because he disappears from his niche and appears to believers in different parts of the world.

In the past war during the North African campaign, "El Niño Perdido" appeared to several soldiers. The mothers of men in the service made promises to the saint so that he would bring their sons home alive. It was to some of these soldiers that the saint appeared. All of them returned. A woman who failed to keep her promise to the saint died suddenly.

(Informant 9. K231.3.)

THE PROTECTION OF THE SAINTS

IN A fiesta held on the 8th (the Fiesta de la Concepción) and the 9th of December, I had a very unusual experience that I still remember vividly although at the time I paid little attention to it.

Six slightly drunk young men and I went out to the plaza. I was a little drunk, too, but I was fully conscious of my acts. We had a liter of mescal. Rather, I had a liter of mescal when the police came and picked up everybody. They took everyone except me. I was left there standing by myself with a glass of liquor in one hand and the liter in the other. The policemen appeared not to see, but I am sure that it was because I invoked the saints' aid.

The same thing happened on the second night. I was with some other friends, and there were seven of us, but the same thing took place. We were walking around the plaza, and I was carrying the liter of mescal. Once more the police came and took everybody. The police looked at me and acted as if they had not seen me. They left me there standing with the liter of liquor in my hand. As I said before, if one invokes the saints, they will protect one.

(Informant 10. D1713.)

ST. ANTHONY PERFORMS A MIRACLE

JUAN MENDOZA, Pedro's father, was a mail carrier in Monterrey, Nuevo León. He was courting the young woman who later became his wife, and on one of his visits to her home she expressed the wish that he become a devout follower of St. Anthony. Juan laughed and said jokingly that St. Anthony was a patron saint for women but not for men.

During the course of the conversation, Juan said, "I wish St. Anthony would do me the miracle of getting me a new pair of trousers."

His sweetheart said, "No, he should punish you because you laughed at my suggestion."

The next day Juan went to deliver the mail. At one of the homes the people had some large dogs. The dogs apparently were not in a very happy mood, and when Juan called to deliver the mail they came out, chased him down the street, and tore the seat of his trousers to shreds. Needless to say, Juan had to buy a new pair.

The next time Juan called at his sweetheart's home, he told her about the dogs and his new pair of trousers.

"Well," she said, "that was St. Anthony's punishment. He had the dogs chase you and tear your trousers, but at the same time he performed the miracle. You have your new pair of trousers."

(Informant 12. D1713.)

THE VIRGIN

SUSIE WORKED in a dry-goods store, and she says that a woman walked in one day and asked for blue satin. There was no blue satin, but there were other blue materials, and Susie showed them to the woman. The woman insisted on blue satin; so Susie asked the reason why it had to be that and nothing else.

"I promised the Virgin," was the reply, "that if my son returned from the war I would dress my little daughter in the habit of the Virgin. The Virgin performed the miracle, and now I must fulfill my promise."

Susie heard everything the woman said, and she suggested, "If you make the habit out of another material, the Virgin will not know."

"Ah, you don't know," the woman replied. "That Virgin is very devilish (cunning)."

(Informant 5.)

THE TRAVELER

A MAN had been traveling from village to village. He was very poor, and no one gave him anything to eat; so he was very hungry.

At last the poor man came to a little house. He knocked at the door and begged for some food. A little old man and a little old lady lived in the little house. The little old lady said, "We are very poor, but come in and eat some little meal cakes."

The man entered and ate with the old couple. When he had finished eating, he went outside and sat on some stones near the house. He picked up one of the rocks and looked at it. Then he threw it away and rose to go. The little old lady came out and gave the poor man some meal cakes so that he could eat them when he was hungry.

The man left, but he returned after a short while. The little old lady came out and said, "Did you forget something?"

The man said, "Yes, I have found something very valuable. You have a great treasure." He told them that there was a gold mine there that would make them very rich. The old couple wanted the man to keep the mine because he had discovered it, but he said, "No, it is yours because you fed me when I was hungry." After saying this the man disappeared, and the old couple were left alone. It was our Lord Jesus Christ whom they had fed.

The old couple became very wealthy. They had all the gold from the mine and lived happily ever after.

(Informant 2. K1811.)

BENITO CÁSAREZ

BENITO CÁSAREZ was madly in love with a young woman. She loved him too, but her father was very strict and would never allow them to see each other. Benito decided to abduct the young woman, but when he went to her bedroom he found her father instead. The man was going to kill Benito, but others intervened and saved him. Benito had to leave the little town.

Time passed, and Benito returned because he loved the young woman very much, but the townspeople arrested him and put him in jail. Benito remained there for a long time, and he was going to be set free, but the day before his release he was murdered.

Benito was an innocent man, and where they buried him a beautiful little tree sprang up and grew. This little tree is always in bloom. The saints proved Benito's innocence.

(Informant 4. E631.0.5.)

REMEDIES

Many people of Mexican ancestry still cling to the belief that supernatural power may induce physical and mental ailments, and they have greater faith in traditional remedies for such ailments than in modern medical treatment.

BOILS

Bath water in which branches of rosemary have been boiled is excellent. Two or three baths are enough to dry up and heal the boils.

CHICKEN POX

In eruptive diseases such as chicken pox, smallpox, and measles, often the afflicted person cannot break out. In such cases a rubdown of lard with sulphur is administered.

COLDS

1. Some saliva rubbed on the sole of the foot will prevent colds after a person has stepped on a cold floor.

2. Baked tomatoes with alcohol or whisky are excellent for rubdowns to cure bad colds.

COLIC

An excellent cure for colic is to place a warm tortilla on the stomach.

DIARRHEA

A herb and whisky treatment is given pregnant women suffering from influenza or diarrhea. A tub is filled with four quarts of whisky, and dried mint leaves, rose leaves, and golden cotula are added to it. After the herbs have soaked for four or six hours, the concoction is strained and into it are dipped new towels which are wrung out and placed over the patient's body. As soon as the towels become warm, they are changed. This treatment is kept up for two or three hours. When the treatment is finished, the patient is given a tea brewed from dried mint leaves, rose leaves, and golden cotula. Whisky is added. Afterwards the patient is covered up and allowed to sleep.

ECZEMA

The best remedy for eczema is potatoes. A man should bury the potatoes without being seen by women. When the potatoes become humid, they are dug up, cut into strips, and applied to the affected parts.

EVIL EYE

The evil eye is an ailment common among small children. It is believed that it is caused by excessive affection. If a woman or a man sees a child with physical attributes which he admires, he must touch the child and invoke God's protection so that the baby will not suffer from the evil eye.

Children seem to be most susceptible to this ailment, although adults may suffer from it occasionally. Babies suffer the direst consequences. They have a very high fever, a lack of appetite and sleep, and usually a swelling on some part of the body. So if a woman casts an evil eye on a child's hand, it will be swollen and red.

In most instances, the cure for evil eye is simple. It consists in passing an unbroken egg over the face and body of the victim, sweeping him, or transferring three mouthfuls of water from the mouth of the person casting the evil eye to the mouth of the victim.

After the cure, precautions must be taken in the disposal

of the egg or eggs used. They must be thrown out in a shady place or buried. If the sun's rays strike them, the evil eye will attack the victim anew. (For evil eye cf. D2071 and D2064.4 in Thompson's *Motif-Index*.)

EVIL EYE (1)

When a person suffers from the evil eye, he says, "I was given the eye." To cure this an unbroken egg is passed over his face. Afterwards, the egg is broken in a saucer, and it is placed under the bed.

Another remedy is to find the person who cast the evil eye and force this person to give the victim three mouthfuls of water.

In order to decide whether a person is suffering from the evil eye, the egg placed under the bed must be examined after the cure has been administered. If a white membraneous film appears over the egg, it means that the person who gave the evil eye is a man. If only an eye appears on the egg, it means that the person who cast the evil eye is a woman.

(Informant 3.)

EVIL EYE (2)

When Chita was small, I took her down town on one occasion. She was a pretty little girl, and people admired her. While I was standing at the counter of one of the department stores, a little Mexican woman approached me and wanted to touch Chita. She said, "What a pretty baby! Won't you let me touch her hair and eyes?"

I didn't like for people to be touching the baby; so I said, "No, please don't touch her!"

The little woman left, and I didn't believe in the evil eye; so I thought no more about it.

The next day Chita became ill. She had a very high fever and was flushed and uneasy. I called the doctor. He came and looked at her. Two or three days went by, and Chita didn't improve. She just seemed to get worse. We went from one doctor to another, but it didn't do any good.

Finally one day my *comadre* Mrs. Ramos came over, and

she looked at Chita and said, "This child is suffering from the evil eye. I can cure her if you will let me try."

I told her to go ahead; and she did. She asked for two eggs and a cup. One of the eggs she passed over Chita's whole face. Then she took the egg, broke it, put it in a cup, stirred it, and made a cross with some of it on Chita's forehead. While doing this she pronounced several prayers. The other egg she placed on the mantelpiece in the living room and asked that no one touch it.

The next day Mrs. Ramos came back. Chita's fever was gone, and you could tell that she was better. Mrs. Ramos then took the egg from the mantelpiece and broke it. If I hadn't been there, I wouldn't believe it, but my husband and I both saw it. The egg looked as if it were hard-boiled. Mrs. Ramos said, "Chita will get well now. The evil eye has gone into the egg; that's why it looks like this."

Chita got well.

(Informant 1.)

EVIL EYE (3)

In my home, whenever anyone became ill my aunt was called.

On one occasion it was believed that my little brother had the evil eye. My aunt came and passed an unbroken egg over my little brother's face. Then she broke the egg, and taking some of it, she made a cross on his forehead. After that she said several prayers and swept my brother from head to foot. She took another egg, broke it, put it in a saucer, and left it under the bed. Later, when my aunt took the egg out from under the bed, she said that she could tell my brother had been suffering from the evil eye because an eye had formed in the egg.

(Informant 17.)

FRIGHT (see Susto)

HEADACHE

1. Ribbons which have been blessed are very effective in curing a headache. The ribbon is tied around the head, and the ache soon disappears.

2. The crushed leaves of vines such as *estrella de Tejas*

(not the same as Texas star) are also used to alleviate headache. The crushed leaves are placed on the temples.

INSANITY

Rice rubbed on the back of an insane person helps restore
sanity.

MEASLES (see Chicken Pox)

PNEUMONIA

Pneumonia is effectively cured by a drink made of cockroaches. Small cockroaches are well toasted, ground, and
added to milk or water to make this drink.

Hot mint tea with lemon is also given to patients suffering from pneumonia.

SMALLPOX (see Chicken Pox)

SORE THROAT

Baked tomatoes are excellent for hoarse and sore throats.

STOMACH OR INTESTINAL INFLAMMATION

Contrayerba (i.e. *Dorstenia contrayerva*), finely ground,
is added to water to alleviate stomach and intestinal inflammation.

Many take the *contrayerba* in slightly sugared water as
a refreshing drink.

STYES

Styes may be cured by passing over them a small pebble
or a doorknob which has collected dew overnight.

SUSTO

Susto is the condition brought about by shock or fright.
It has many causes, such as the announcement of good or
bad news, accidents, or any startling occurrence. Cures for
fright vary, but the most popular seem to be these:

1. Teas brewed from different leaves are given the patient. Sometimes a gold ring, a piece of red ribbon, or a clod
of clay from the chimney is added to the tea.

2. Water sweetened with sugar or water with a little
vinegar and salt is given to the patient.

3. The patient is swept from head to foot while a certain
number of credos are repeated.

SUSTO (1)

On one of my visits to the home of an informant, Mrs.

Cecilia G. Vda. de Hernández, I witnessed the curing of Lily Hernández, her daughter. The treatment lasted three days, and Mrs. Hernández administered it. It was begun on Friday afternoon soon after my arrival.

First Mrs. Hernández went out to the kitchen and placed a small *comal* (a flat iron grill for cooking tortillas) on the stove. Then she placed a lump of alum on the comal and came back into the bedroom. She made Lily undress and lie face down on the bed with her arms outstretched in the form of a cross. Then covering Lily with a sheet and taking a small broom made of green twigs and shaped in the form of a cross, Mrs. Hernández proceeded to sweep Lily from head to foot. As she swept, Mrs. Hernández recited three credos. After this she took me out to the kitchen, where we looked at the alum. Something resembling foam had risen to the surface, and Mrs. Hernández gazed intently and then asked me to look at it.

"Don't you see the forms of two men fighting?" she asked.

"Well, yes," I hesitated, "but it's not very clear. Won't you show me exactly where it is that you see those two forms?"

She peered down and patiently outlined what appeared to be two forms of men with outstretched arms and doubled fists.

"I thought that was what had shocked Lily and now I am sure," she said. "She never told me, but I found out that a man tried to assault her and her boy friend. Her boy friend had to fight with this other man, and it frightened Lily very much."

Mrs. Hernández then gave Lily a tea that she had brewed, and I left after obtaining permission to come back to witness the rest of the cure.

On Saturday afternoon I returned. Mrs. Hernández again placed the alum on the stove, swept Lily just as she had done on the previous day, and gave her some more tea. Then Mrs. Hernández and I went to look at the alum. She was very pleased.

"The cure is going to be very effective," she said. "Today, the figures of the men are barely visible."

When she asked me about it, I affirmed her statement.

On Sunday afternoon the cure was completed. As she had done previously, Mrs. Hernández placed the alum on the stove and swept Lily from head to foot, but she did not give her any tea. After this she said that she would be gone for a short time. I noticed a small bundle under her arm, but I did not ask what it contained. About forty-five minutes later she reappeared and told what she had done.

"I had to take the lingerie that Lily was wearing on the day when she was frightened to the exact location where the attempted assault took place," she explained. "I have dragged the lingerie across the exact spot three times in one direction and three times in another so as to form the sign of the cross. Now I shall put the lingerie on her, and we shall know whether the cure is complete or not."

She then dressed Lily in the lingerie, and we sat and chatted amiably for about half an hour. She asked Lily how she felt, and she replied that she was sweating profusely. Mrs. Hernández covered her with a blanket, and immediately afterwards we went into the kitchen to look at the alum. Nothing could be seen.

"I am very happy," said Mrs. Hernández. "The two men who were visible on the first and second day have disappeared, and that means that the cure is successful."

When I left, Lily was asleep, but she was still sweating profusely. Now Lily is well and has returned to her work.

(Informant 2.)

SUSTO (2)

We have eight children. When they were small we counted them whenever we went out: one, two, three, four, five, six, seven, and eight.

One day after going for a drive with the children, we came home and started to put them to bed. About an hour and a half passed before we finished. I counted them: one, two, three, four, five, six, seven. One was missing. I ran downstairs and called to my husband, "Daddy, one of our children is missing!"

He ran out of the house and went out to the garage.

There, in the car, he found María Ester, whom we had left locked up.

María Ester was only three years old, and she had cried until her eyes were almost swollen shut. She said, "Daddy, when you closed the door, I screamed and told you to let me out."

We took her in the house and hugged her, kissed her, and cried over her. We tried to comfort her and finally we put her to bed.

From that day on, María Ester did not eat or sleep well. We took her from one doctor to another, but it did no good. Then one day Mrs. Ramos came to see me, and she asked what was wrong with the baby. I told her, and she said, "She is frightened, but I'll cure her if you'll have faith."

I promised I would. We went upstairs. Mrs. Ramos brewed a tea and gave it to María Ester. Then she undressed her and laid her facedown on the bed with her arms outstretched in the form of a cross. We covered María Ester up, and Mrs. Ramos went out to the garage. About forty-five minutes later, the baby began to sweat. Suddenly, she raised her little head and said, "Mommy, did you call me?"

"No! I didn't call you," I replied.

She lay down; I covered her, and she continued to sweat. Then she asked again, "Mommy, did you call me?"

"No!" I said.

"I heard you call me," María insisted.

She went to sleep, but she woke again and asked, "Mommy, what do you want?"

"María Ester, what is the matter? I haven't called you."

When Mrs. Ramos came back from the garage, she said that she had been praying in the car where María Ester had been locked up.

"Did María Ester act as if someone had called her?" she asked.

"Yes," I said, "she did, but I didn't call her."

"I called her three times," Mrs. Ramos said.

María Ester recovered.

(Informant 16.)

WARTS

1. Warts may be removed with freshly cooked pinto beans. The beans are crushed and the soft meat is spread over the wart.

2. Strips of potatoes applied directly to the warts are said to be effective.

3. Throw a grain of salt into the fire and try to run out of the room before it pops. If you succeed, your warts will disappear.

BELIEFS AND SUPERSTITIONS

MOST PEOPLE of Mexican ancestry are strongly influenced by traditional beliefs and superstitions, though this influence seems to be declining among the younger generation in the United States.

CHILDREN

If a woman marries, she should have as many children as God grants her. If she does not, she will be punished. God will come back to judge the world, and when He does He will question each woman as to the number of children each bore. If a woman was supposed to bear twelve children but bore only ten, God will tell her to go and look for the souls of the other two. A woman will not be able to enter Heaven until she has found them. (Q251.)

CROSS

1. Four persons meeting and unconsciously forming the sign of the cross while exchanging greetings will have good luck. If any one of the four is single, it means that he or she will be married within a year.

2. A small cross hung above a door will keep out evil spirits.

3. Many people make the sign of the cross to avert hailstorms. A cross is drawn on the ground, and it is outlined with ashes. It is made in the direction of the oncoming storm. (D1766.6.)

CROWS

Crows seen in pairs are an omen of good luck.

Crows seen in odd numbers are an omen of bad luck. (B147.1.1.1.)

DEAD

Persons should not speak ill of the dead. The dead may return to punish them. (E235.1.)

DEATH (see Owls)

Owls hooting or screeching at night presage death in the family. (B147.1.1.4.)

To offset death, all shoes should be turned upside down when an owl is heard screeching.

DREAMS

A person who dreams that he or she is crying will be very happy. (D1812.3.3.)

EARS

Burning of the ears means that someone is speaking ill of the person whose ears burn.

ECLIPSES

1. Eclipses are believed to be caused by the Devil or by collisions between the sun and the moon. (A737.)

2. It is a common belief that women who are pregnant when there is an eclipse may give birth to deformed children. Harelip is usually thought to be an effect of an eclipse. (D1812.5.1.4.)

FINGERNAILS

Baby fingernails should not be cut, because cutting shortens the life span of the child or impairs his eyesight.

White spots on the fingernails indicate the number of women or men friends a person has.

GOOD LUCK (see Crows and Spiders)

Two persons who speak at the same time will live another year.

HARELIP (see Eclipses)

HOLY WATER

Some people take water to church to be blessed. It is put away, and when a storm threatens, the people go out and throw handfuls of the holy water at the clouds. The water is believed to avert a serious storm or to drive it away completely. (V132.)

KNIVES

People take knives and brandish them at the storm clouds in order to drive them away.

MARRIAGE (see Cross and Thread)

Single persons who sit at the head of the table will remain single.

MISCARRIAGES

Women who suffer miscarriages will hear their children crying for them.

MONEY

If your nose or right hand itches, you will receive money.

OWLS (see Death)

If a person is bewitched, owls will fly past the house and whistle.

POTIONS

A husband's love may be kept by putting two drops of a potion in his coffee or milk. The potion is prepared by boiling his dirty socks in water. (D1242.2.)

SALT

To avert bad luck, a person should throw a pinch of salt over the left shoulder.

SPELLS

A spell may be cast on a group by the burial of a humming bird at midnight. (D1273.) The following tale presents an example. The Tiger baseball club had been playing against Lockhart's baseball team, but the Tigers were never able to beat Lockhart. The Lockhart baseball club had cast a spell on the Tigers by burying a humming bird under first base in the home stadium of the Tigers. The humming bird was buried exactly at midnight. Since then, the Tigers have lost all the games they have played with Lockhart.

Physical illness is very frequently attributed to spells. These are believed to be cast by enemies. The following two stories are illustrative.

SPELLS (1)

Luis Rojo made his living by playing his accordion in bars and saloons. At one of the saloons he met a girl and got into trouble with her. When the mother of the girl demanded that Luis marry her, he refused. Luis said that she went with other men, and he would not marry her.

One day the girl invited Luis to have coffee at her house. She said that her mother had forgiven him, and Luis accepted. After drinking a cup, he felt certain that the girl's mother had put something in his coffee to cast a spell on him. From then on he suffered with stomach trouble.

Finally Luis went to a woman in New Braunfels. She told him that a spell had been placed on him. To get rid of the spell and his stomach trouble, Luis must eat garlic every day for the next five years. Luis has been eating his garlic faithfully for four years.

(Informant 18.)

SPELLS (2)

Susie told me that María Mendez married a man whom she loved very much. His family did not like her.

One day when María went to see her in-laws, they became very angry and told her that they were going to put her under a spell. At the same time, they threw a handful of white powder on her. María became hysterical. Susie tried to explain that no one could cast a spell, but María would not listen. Susie even wet her finger and tasted some of the powder to find out what it was. It was table salt. She told María, but María would not believe her. María lost her appetite, and she could not sleep. A year ago María died from tuberculosis, but she always believed that the spell had caused her illness.

(Informant 19.)

SPIDERS

Spiders with six or eight legs predict good news and good luck.

Spiders with five or seven legs predict bad news and bad luck.

STORMS (see Cross, Holy Water, and Knives)

SWALLOWS

Swallows should not be handled. If they are, great care should be taken to see that the hands are not carried to the head immediately. Otherwise, baldness will result.

Swallows are sacred and should not be killed. People hold that the swallow plucked the thorns from Jesus's forehead when He was crucified. (A2221.2.4.)

THREAD

Stray pieces of thread on a person's clothing indicate an early marriage or a happy remembrance of the person on the part of friends. A long white piece of thread indicates that the future bride or bridegroom is tall and blond. A short dark piece of thread indicates that he or she is short and dark haired.

If the piece of thread is wound around the finger and each time it is wound a letter of the alphabet is repeated, the letter on which the thread is wound out is the initial of the first name of the person thinking of one or that of the future bride or bridegroom.

WARTS

A person who comes to the house during a meal must be invited to partake of the food. If he is not invited and craves some of the food, a wart will grow on the tip of his tongue.

PROVERBS AND SAYINGS

A boca cerrada no entra mosca.

Flies do not enter a closed mouth. A closed mouth catches no flies.

A buen hambre no hay mal pan.

To a good appetite no bread is bad. Hunger is the best sauce.

A mí de la gallina me gusta el ala (Lala) y del mar me gusta la ola (Lola).

I like the wing of the chicken and the wave of the sea. This saying loses its meaning and significance in translation because its value lies in the play on words. "El ala" and "la ola" are pronounced rapidly and become "Lala" and "Lola," names of women.

Ahora es cuando, yerbabuena, le has de dar sabor al caldo.

Now, mint, is when you must give the soup flavor. Strike while the iron is hot. Now's your chance.

Al haber gallinas hay gallos.

Where there are hens there are cocks. Sugar draws flies.

Al mal paso, darle prisa.
  Hurry over a bad road. When the going is bad, hurry.
  The sooner, the better.
Al que le apriete el zapato, que se lo afloje.
  He whose shoe pinches him should loosen it. The foot
  best knows where the shoe pinches. The wearer best
  knows where the shoe wrings him.
Al que le duela la muela, que se la saque.
  He whose molar hurts should have it taken out. This
  expression has the same meaning as the one above.
Al que no le guste el juste, que lo tire y monte en pelo.
  He who does not like the saddle may throw it away and
  ride bareback. Take it or leave it. Here the word *juste*
  replaces the correct *fuste*.
Arrieros somos y por el camino andamos.
  We are mule drivers and we are walking on the road.
  We are human beings and walk along the road of life
  together. We are all in the same boat.
Cada loco con su tema.
  Every madman to his own theme. There is method in his
  madness.
Cada oveja con su pareja.
  Every sheep with its partner. Birds of a feather flock to-
  gether.
Cada pobrete lo que tiene mete.
  Every poor man contributes what he has. To put in one's
  two cents' worth.
Cincuenta años en la marina y no conoce una ballena.
  Fifty years in the navy and he doesn't know a whale.
Como moscas a la miel.
  Like flies to the honey.
Cuando ven el palo caído todos quieren hacer leña.
  When people see a fallen tree, all want to make firewood.
  The tree is no sooner down but everyone runs for his
  hatchet. This expression is applied to people who begin to
  take advantage of someone who has suffered misfortune.
Da y ten, y harás bien.
  Give and take and you will do good. Be liberal but pru-
  dent. Give and spend and God will send.

Dar atole con el dedo.

To give gruel with the finger. To deceive with words or acts, especially to deceive one's husband.

Dar gato por liebre.

To give a cat for a hare. To deceive, to cheat.

De tal palo tal astilla.

Chip off the old block. Like father, like son.

Díme con quien andas y te diré quien eres.

Tell me with whom you associate and I will tell you who you are. A man is known by the company he keeps.

Dios los creó y ellos se juntan.

God created them and they get (or flock) together.

¿De dónde vienes y para dónde vas?

¿Cómo te llamas y con quién estás?

Respuesta:
Vengo de misa,
Voy para casa,
Estoy con un burro,
Y me llamo Tomasa.

Question: Where are you coming from and where are you going?/ What is your name and who is with you?/ I am coming from church,/ I am going home,/ I am with an ass,/ And my name is Tomasa. Children use this rhymed question and answer to taunt someone who has asked an impertinent question. In the last line of the reply, the name of the inquisitive child may be substituted although the majority just say *Tomasa* to rhyme with *casa*. An English rhyme similar to this would be: What's your name?/ Puddin' Tame,/ Ask me again,/ And I'll tell you the same.

El flojo y el mezquino dos veces andan el camino.

The lazy and the stingy walk the same road twice.

El hábito no hace al monje.

The habit does not make the monk. Clothes do not make the man.

El hombre pone y Dios dispone.

Man proposes, God disposes.

El pan ajeno hace al hijo bueno.

The bread of another makes the son good. He who has

to work for his bread appreciates what he had at his father's table.

El pecado se dice pero el pecador no.

The sin may be told but not the sinner's name.

El primer pensamiento es el mejor.

The first thought is the best.

El que boca tiene a Roma va.

He who has a mouth goes to Rome. He who speaks is heard.

El que la hace la paga.

He who does it will pay for it.

El que no habla nadie le oye.

He who does not speak is not heard.

El que no quiere ruido que no críe cochinos.

He who doesn't want noise should not raise hogs. Don't make trouble if you don't want trouble.

El que no se arriesga no pasa la mar.

He who takes no risks will never cross the sea. Nothing venture, nothing gain.

El que para tonto nace hasta guaje no para.

He who is born (to be) a fool will not stop until he becomes an (empty) gourd. He who is born a fool is never cured. Once a fool, always a fool. The *guaje* is a dry empty gourd; it is often used to keep a person afloat in water.

El que por su cuenta es buey hasta la coyunda lame.

He who allows himself to be made into an ox will even lick the (yoking) straps. He who allows himself to be made into a cuckold must wear the horns.

El que solo vive solo muere.

He who lives alone dies alone.

El que tiene buen voto se hinca a cualquier santo.

He who has a good votive offering may kneel to any saint.

En la tardanza está el peligro.

The danger lies in the delay.

En martes ni te cases ni te embarques.

Do not marry or board a ship on Tuesday. The superstitious beliefs Mexicans associate with Tuesday correspond to those Americans associate with Friday.

Entre la espada y la pared.

> Between the sword and the wall. Between the devil and the deep blue sea.

Entre menos burros, más elotes.

> The fewer donkeys, the more cobs. The fewer, the better (cheer). *Elotes* (corn cobs), dried as well as green, are given burros to eat.

Hablen del rey de Roma y pronto la cabeza asoma.

> Speak of the king of Rome, and he soon shows his head. Talk of an angel and you'll hear his wings.

Hablando del diablo pronto la cabeza asoma.

> Speak of the Devil, he soon shows his head. Speak of the Devil and he will appear.

Hacer de uno cera y pábilo.

> To make wax and candlewick out of anyone. To twist a person around one's little finger.

Hasta que te cases, mira lo que haces.

> Until you marry, watch what you do. Until you marry, watch your step.

Hay muchachos viejos y viejos muchachos.

> There are young men who are old and old men who are young. Some young men are old, some old men are young.

Hay muertos que no hacen ruido y son sus penas mayores.

> There are dead men who make no noise and their sorrows are greater. This saying is applied to secretive or hypocritical persons whose true character is discovered by accident.

Haz bien y no mires a quien.

> Do good and don't see whom you do it to. Do good and shame the Devil.

Ir por lana y volver trasquilado.

> To go for wool and come out shorn.

Juntos pero no revueltos.

> Together but not mixed.

La limpieza no está reñida con la pobreza.

> Cleanliness has not fallen out with poverty. Poverty is no excuse for uncleanliness.

La luna no es queso porque se ve redonda.

> The moon is not cheese because it looks round. Appearances are deceiving.

La necesidad es la madre de la invención.
Necessity is the mother of invention.

La necesidad tiene cara de hereje.
Necessity (poverty) has the face of a heretic. Beggars aren't welcome.

Las doce en punto y el buey arando.
It is twelve o'clock and the ox is (still) plowing. It is twelve o'clock and all is well.

Las doce han dado y el gato armado.
It is twelve o'clock and the cat (is) armed. This means that people have been engaged in a particular activity for hours but the end is not in sight.

Le dan en el codo y aprieta la mano.
They ask him for some money and he closes his hand.

Lo que se hereda no se hurta.
What is inherited is not stolen.

Los golpes hacen al jinete.
Hard knocks make the rider. Practice makes perfect.

Los muertos al pozo y los vivos al negocio.
The dead to the grave and the living to their business. Let the dead bury the dead.

Más vale andar solo que mal acompañado.
It is better to walk alone than in bad company.

Más vale malo por conocido que bueno por conocer.
Better a known evil than an unknown good.

Más vale pájaro en mano que dos volando.
A bird in the hand is better than two flying. A bird in the hand is worth two in the bush.

Más vale pobre que solo.
It is better to be poor than to be alone.

Más vale sucio en casa y no limpio en el camposanto.
It is better to be dirty at home than clean in the cemetery. It is better not to overwork and live longer than to overwork and die quickly.

Más vale tarde que nunca.
Better late than never.

Más vale tuerto que ciego.
Better to be half blind than all blind.

Más vale maña que fuerza.

Craft is better than force.

Nadie sabe el bien que tiene hasta que lo ha perdido.

No one knows the good he has until he has lost it.

Nadie sabe para quien trabaja.

No one knows for whom he works. This expression means that persons who leave money and goods never know who will enjoy what they leave behind.

Ni tanto que queme al santo, ni tanto que no le alumbre.

Not so much candlelight as will burn the saint, nor so little as will leave him in the dark. Be moderate.

No es tan bravo el león como lo pintan.

The lion is not as fierce as he is pictured to be. The Devil is not so black as he is painted.

No le busques tres patas al gato porque le encuentras cuatro.

Do not look for three of the cat's paws because you will find four. Do not look for trouble, because you will find it. Let sleeping dogs lie.

No hay mal que por bien no venga, ni enfermedad que dure cien años.

There is no evil that does not bring some good with it nor illness that lasts a hundred years. It's an ill wind that blows no good.

No hay más amigo que Dios ni más pariente que un peso.

There is no better friend than God nor better relative than a peso.

No tener ni saliva.

Not even to have saliva. Poor as a church mouse.

No todos los que chiflan son arrieros.

Not all who whistle are mule drivers. This saying means that appearances are deceiving.

Ojos que no ven, corazón que no siente.

Eyes that see not, heart that feels not. What the eye sees not, the heart rues not. Out of sight, out of mind.

Panza llena, corazón contento.

A full belly, a happy heart. When the belly is full, the bones are at rest.

Para eso son los bienes, para remediar los males.

Goods are for this, to remedy evils.

Parece que no quiebra un plato, y todos los tiene mochos.

It seems as if she wouldn't break a plate, but all her plates are chipped. It seems as if butter wouldn't melt in her mouth. This expression is used in speaking of a person who seems to be very innocent but is not.

Perro que ladra no muerde.

Barking dogs don't bite.

Pobre del pobre que al cielo no va

Lo friegan aquí y lo friegan allá.

He is poor indeed who does not go to heaven; they beat him here and they will beat him there.

Quien todo lo quiere, todo lo pierde.

He who wants everything loses everything. He who covets all loses all. Want all, lose all.

Sacar dinero hasta de las piedras.

To get money even out of the rocks. To squeeze blood out of a turnip.

Tener suerte de gato boca arriba.

To have the luck of a cat (who lands) mouth right side up. To land on your feet.

Tonto y rudo pero pesudo.

Stupid and unpolished but rich.

Traigo bastón en la mano y frecuento la fiscalía,

Me llamo Don Apolonio y me apellido García.

I carry a cane in my hand and I visit the Ministerial office frequently, my name is Don Apolonio and my surname is García. This expression is used to show contempt for persons who pry into other's affairs or who attach undue importance to themselves. The surname García seems to be used only for the sake of rhyme.

Un garbanzo de a libra.

A chick pea that weighs one pound. This expression is used referring to a rare or unusual occurrence.

Un peso vale más que cien consejos.

A peso is worth more than a hundred counsels.

RIDDLES

Baila pero no en la *harina.*
    She dances but not upon the flour.

                    Solution: Bailarina—dancer.

Blanca como la nieve,
    Prieta como el carbón,
    Anda y no tiene pies,
    Habla y no tiene boca.

White as the snow,
Black as the coal,
She walks and she has no feet,
She speaks and she has no mouth.

                    Solution: Una carta—a letter.

Blanco fué mi nacimiento,
    Me pintaron de colores,
    He causado muchas muertes,
    Y he empobrecido señores.

At birth I was white,
But I was painted with colors,
I have caused many deaths,
And impoverished many men.

                    Solution: Barajas—cards.

Caballito de banda en banda que ni come ni bebe ni anda.
    A little horse that neither eats, drinks, nor canters (takes
    you) from one bank of the river to the other.

                    Solution: El puente—the bridge.

Dentro del *mar* está un queso,
    Dentro del *queso* está una O,
    Dentro de la O está una *T,*
    Adivínemela Ud.

In the sea there is a cheese,
In the cheese there is an O,
In the O there is a T,
Tell me what it is!

                    Solution: Marquesote—sponge cake.

Entré a la iglesia,
    Pisé una *grada,*

Volteé para atrás,
Y no ví *nada.*

I entered the church,
I stepped upon a flagstone,
I turned around,
And I saw nothing.

> Solution: Granada—pomegranate.

Lana sube, *lana baja.*
Wool goes up, wool comes down.

> Solution: La navaja—the knife.
> (*B* and *v* are pronounced the same.)

Plata no es,
  Oro no es,
  ¿Qué es?

It is not silver,
It is not gold,
What is it?

> Solution: Plátano—banana.

Rita, Rita que en el monte grita
  Y en la casa está silencita.

Rita, Rita shouts in the forest
And at home she is silent.

> Solution: El hacha—the ax.

Una vaca negra pasó por el mar pegando bramidos sin ser
animal.
A black cow bellowing passed over the sea although she
was not an animal.

> Solution: La nube—the thundercloud.

Una vieja larga que le escurre la manteca,
  ¿Qué es?
Who is the tall old woman whose garments drip fat?

> Solution: La vela—the candle.

Ya ves cuan claro es,
  Adivíname lo que es.

You see how clear it is,
Tell me what it is.

> Solution: Llaves—keys.

Wilson M. Hudson, *born in Texas, was taken by his parents to Tampico at an early age. When he was brought out of Mexico after the Carrancista revolution, he spoke a mixture of Spanish and English without knowing they were different languages. He received his higher education at the universities of Texas and Chicago. He has taught English at The Rice Institute and The University of Chicago, and he is now teaching at The University of Texas.*

TO WHOM GOD WISHES TO GIVE HE WILL GIVE

By Wilson M. Hudson

In 1932 I heard this tale told by a blind shepherd in the mountains of western Jalisco.

In Spain and Spanish America stories of two friends or two brothers, one rich and the other poor, are numerous and widespread. The poor man deceives the rich one and wins money from him, and often the rich man loses his life. The folktale that follows is unusual in that the poor man uses no trickery at all, but relies on the saying that he loves to repeat. He happens to stop a runaway horse and so gain the gratitude of El Gran Señor, the Lord Himself; and the treasure that El Gran Señor reveals is the kind that can be removed only by the poor man or by someone in his presence. The rich friend, through his greed, becomes the means of transporting this treasure, temporarily transformed into mud (or something worse), to the poor man's hut. Thus the often-repeated saying comes true.

The Texas Folklore Society has published at least four other stories about two compadres, all involving deception: three by Riley Aiken in "A Pack Load of Mexican Tales" (Publication XII [1935]), and one by Wilson M. Hudson (Publication XXI [1946]). For a general discussion of folktales of this kind, see the comparative notes on Nos. 172-176 in Espinosa's *Cuentos Españoles*.

This was a lazy man who had an energetic man for his compadre.

One morning the energetic man, who owned a store, told his wife to carry a message to his compadre.

"Tell him," he said, "I want him to pay his account. It is long past due and I am tired of waiting. If he cannot pay, let him come over and help me haul some rocks, and I will give him credit for his work."

When he heard this message, the lazy man said, "I have no money and your rocks are too heavy for me. Tell my compadre not to worry about this little account. To whom God wishes to give He will give even if He has to put it in through the window."

It was the habit of this lazy man not to get up before ten o'clock in the morning. Usually his wife gave him breakfast in bed so that he would not have to make the effort of dressing himself at so early an hour.

One day the spring near his house dried up, and he was forced to go higher on the mountain to look for another one. While walking along a dim trail he heard hoofbeats rapidly coming nearer. As he stepped off the trail he saw a runaway horse mounted by a señor in elegant dress with a flowing white beard.

Without taking thought, he reached out and grasped the horse's bit and stopped him. The rider thanked him with dignity for his courage and presence of mind, saying that he would reward him by revealing the hiding place of a *tatema*.

A *tatema* is a buried treasure that can be found only by supernatural aid and that can be taken out of hiding only by the person to whom it is revealed or by others in his presence and with his permission.

Taking the lazy man to one side of the trail, the dignified stranger said, "Move that flat rock and underneath it you will find a treasure covered with oak leaves."

As the man was moving the stone, the rider and horse suddenly disappeared. The lazy man brushed the oak leaves aside with his hands and discovered six chests. He opened one and saw that it was filled with silver coins. At this point his natural laziness began to overcome him. He put some coins into his pocket, only sixteen to be exact, because more would have been too heavy to carry along.

When he got home, he lay down on his bed to refresh himself with a good siesta. Late in the afternoon when he arose to eat supper he felt the weight of the coins in his pocket.

"Wife," he said, "take these to my compadre and pay my account."

The energetic compadre was greatly surprised to see the money because he could not imagine that the lazy compadre had worked to earn it. Being very curious, he decided to visit his compadre and learn whatever he could.

Early the next morning he went to his friend's house, but he had to wait until the lazy man awoke at his usual ten o'clock. When the energetic one asked about the money, the lazy compadre told him exactly what had happened the day before.

"But why," asked the energetic compadre, "didn't you bring more of the money?"

"It was too heavy, much too heavy," said the lazy man. "If you will pack it back for me on your mules, I will give you one half of everything in the boxes. To whom God wishes to give He will give even if He has to put it in through the window."

This proposal was eagerly accepted by the energetic compadre, and it was agreed that they should leave at eleven o'clock in order to reach the flat stone by the trail at midnight. They were to start from the house of the lazy man so that he would not have to walk.

In the meantime this lazy man lay down for a rest, asking his wife not to disturb him until eleven o'clock. At that time she woke him up and told him that his compadre had not come; yet he did not get up, saying that he supposed his friend would come later. At twelve o'clock the wife woke him again in a state of alarm. She tried to stir him up by telling him that his compadre might go alone and take all the treasure for himself.

"Lie down and go to sleep," said the lazy man. "I am tired and I will not get up at this time of night. To whom God wishes to give He will give even if He has to put it in through the window."

The wife had good reason to be afraid. The energetic man had asked himself why he should divide the treasure with his compadre, who had gained it by little if any exertion. He said to himself that he had been a hard worker all of his life and that for this reason he had mules and his lazy friend had none. Besides, how could such a lazy man make proper use of the great fortune?

So the energetic man went with his mules and his servants to the flat rock by the trail. The servants brushed aside the leaves and opened the chests; but instead of a multitude of coins they found a mass of foul-smelling mud.

The energetic man was so disappointed and angry that he decided to take vengeance on his lazy compadre. He ordered his drivers to load the chests on the backs of the mules.

At two in the morning he arrived with his cargo at his compadre's hut. He gave orders to empty the contents of the chests in front of the door and by the window. The lazy man and his wife were sound asleep and heard nothing.

In the morning the wife arose at her customary hour and tried to open the door. She could not—some great weight was holding it shut. Nor could she budge the window. She roused her husband and together they were able to push the wooden window ajar.

Immediately a shower of silver coins poured through the crack and into the room.

"See, wife," said the lazy man. "What did I tell you? To whom God wishes to give He will give even if He has to put it in through the window."

They opened the window a little more, and more coins came in. Finally they swung it open all the way. From the pile of coins inside, the wife pulled herself through the window onto another pile outside. At the door she saw a great heap of coins as high as the latch.

With encouragement from her husband and little real help, she carried all of the coins into the hut. Then she prepared a meal for him—he felt obliged to return to bed after all this disturbance. Here he was given breakfast by his wife. Then he told her to take some of the coins to his compadre's store and buy a good supply of food and some much-needed clothing.

When the energetic man was paid with the same kind of coins sent before by his lazy friend, he did not know what to think. He asked whether his compadre had made another trip to the hiding place of the treasure.

The wife told him that the door and the window had been blocked in the night with great piles of coins.

"My compadre was right," said the man, trying to conceal his surprise. "To whom God wishes to give He will give even if He has to put it in through the window."

THE FISHERMAN AND THE SNAKE OF MANY COLORS

By WILSON M. HUDSON

THIS TALE was told in 1940 by Señora Cecilia Cortés of Ameca, Jalisco. She believed that it was a true account of a series of events that had taken place in her town.

The story does not readily fit into any of the recognized patterns of the folktale. Certain folk motifs are no doubt present, but it is not easy to identify them exactly. The priest's explanation, stated in the text below, is that the fisherman had given his soul to the devil and that the devil had come to live with him in the form of a snake. The devil as a snake (G303.3.3.15) is of course very common, and snake paramours (B613.1) are far from unusual. It may be that the story involves a liaison between a mortal and a water spirit (F420.6.1). The fisherman undergoes a transformation (D190) after he enters the river to live with the snake. He becomes a kind of water demon that drags people under the surface, but he is still mortal, as shown by the fact that he grows older and weaker with the passage of time.

Apparently the name Chavarín has no particular significance in connection with the story.

IN AMECA, a town in Jalisco northwest of Guadalajara, there lived a fisherman who had a very bad reputation. He was married but childless. The people of Ameca called him El Chavarín.

One day El Chavarín had been casting his net from early morning until late afternoon without luck. He was angry to think that he had fished so long without taking anything.

"*Carray!*" he exclaimed. "I shall cast the net only one

The priest invoked God's name and began to sprinkle
El Chavarín and the snake with holy water.

more time. If I don't catch anything, the devil is going to pay for it."

He cast the net and drew it out. It was empty except for one small snake. This snake was covered with many vivid colors—it was beautiful. At once El Chavarín felt a fondness for it. He resolved to take it home with him.

Not wanting to answer questions that his wife might ask, he placed the snake in the *tapanco* or loft of his hut. Every day he would feed the snake and caress it, and every day it became larger and larger. Now El Chavarín loved the snake. At night he would leave his wife below and sleep in the *tapanco* with the snake twined about his arm or his leg.

The wife began to wonder why her husband wished to sleep in the *tapanco* away from her. Could it be possible that in some fashion he had concealed another woman there? One night she climbed to the *tapanco* herself and found her husband fast asleep with a large colored snake wound about his arm, its head resting against his cheek.

In a great fright she rushed off to see the priest. When she made him understand what she had seen, he returned to the hut with her, bringing a bowl of holy water and a candle that had been blessed at the altar. The wife and the priest went up into the *tapanco* and found El Chavarín and the snake sleeping together just as the wife had said. While the wife held the burning holy candle, the priest invoked God's name and began to sprinkle El Chavarín and the snake with holy water. In a searing flash and a shattering explosion, El Chavarín and the snake disappeared.

The wife and the priest rushed into the street along with everybody else in the neighborhood. They could all hear the voice of El Chavarín down by the river screaming out all kinds of horrible blasphemies. After a while the voice ceased and El Chavarín was heard no more that night.

The priest explained that El Chavarín was of such a bad heart that he had given his soul into the hands of the devil, who had come to live with him in the form of a snake.

This was not the end of El Chavarín. After his disappearance, drownings became frequent in the Ameca River. It was the custom of women to wash clothes on the rocks along the bank. Whenever one of them would enter the deeper water, she would go down never to be seen again.

One day a woman was bathing in the river feeling secure because her husband was there beside her. Suddenly she began to sink, but her husband grabbed her by the hand and pulled her out. She said that someone had pulled her down by the ankle, and when he looked he saw that she bore the marks of five human fingers.

The drownings usually happened in the late afternoon. The women learned to do their washing well before that time. Fewer of them were drowned, but now and then a stubborn boy would go for a swim and never come out.

Some policemen were placed on duty by the river and told to shoot at anything suspicious in the water; but their time was lost, because El Chavarín would never come to the surface.

When people learned to stay away from the river, El Chavarín gave no more trouble. Yet on one occasion someone actually saw him.

An old man, Pedro Ortiz, was once cutting grass along the river for his burros. He became tired and straightened up to rest his back. On the bank below him a willow tree grew straight out over the water. Something in the tree caught Pedro's eye. What was it? It was covered with hair and was resting on the trunk, propped up on a limb. The hair was so long that it trailed in the water. In a moment Pedro could make out two human feet dangling down into the current with hair swirling about them. It was El Chavarín!

Pedro reached for his machete with the hope of being able to strike at least one blow. He moved very slowly towards the tree, but just as he was drawing back his arm, a large snake with vivid colors fell from a limb above El Chavarín and woke him. El Chavarín gave Pedro a look of blazing hatred and slipped into the water. The snake swam around in a circle and then disappeared beneath the surface too.

Pedro said that El Chavarín's long hair was white. This led people to believe that El Chavarín had become old. It is true that he is no longer strong, for women again wash their clothes in the river without being drawn under and even a boy can kick loose from his grasp.

INDEX

Aarne, Antti, 72, 80, 81
Aiken, Riley, "A Pack Load of Mexican Tales," 128
Alice, Texas, 9, 15, 42
All Souls' Day, 17, 18, 63, 66, 68
Anthony, St., 104
Applegate, Frank, *Native Tales of New Mexico*, 2
Arnold, Matthew, 3
Asthma, 54

Bard, Father Peter, 16, 60, 61
Barrera, Juan García, 20-22
Barrie, J. M., *Rosalind*, 6
Bath, as a cure, 13, 25, 35-36, 39, 44, 45, 50, 53, 55, 58-59
bear, 100
Beeville, 25
"Beliefs and Superstitions," 114-118
bell, church, 60-62
Beltrán, José, 3
Billy the Kid, 2
blindness, 56
Boatright, Mody C., v
Boggs, Ralph S., 72, 84, 86
Bowie, Jim, 2
Bowlegs, 51
Brownsville, 15, 27
Brujo, 16, 31, 32
bull, 3, 4-5
buried treasure, 96-102, 128-132

Canales, Don Albino, 14, 23, 40
Canales, Don Andrés, 11, 14, 20, 22
Canales, Don Andrés, son, 23
Canales, Florencio García, 20
Canales, Señora Gertrudis C. de, 20
Canales, Don Jesús, 20
Canales, Judge José, 22
Canales, Doña Tomasita, 22-24
Catarrh, 54
Catholic faith, 24
Cenizo, 19

Charco, in Goliad County, 55
"Charm in Mexican Folktales," by J. Frank Dobie, 1-8
Cisneros, José, v, 48, 75, 82, 133
Clubfeet, 52
Coffee, used in a cure, 43
Concepcion, in Duval County, 49
Corpus Christi, 13, 20, 21, 25, 36
Coyotes, 6
Cripple, 51-52
Crockett, David, 2
Cures, 18-68, 106-114

Devil, 86-90, 132
Dinero, in Live Oak County, 55
Dobie, J. Frank, v; "Charm in Mexican Folktales," 1-8; *The Longhorns*, 3-5; *Tongues of the Monte*, 7-8; 10, 50
Dodson, Ruth, v; "Don Pedrito Jaramillo: The Curandero of Los Olmos," 9-70
Dorson, Richard, 2
Drinking, 49-50

Epileptic, 37-38
Espinosa, A. M., 72, 84, 128
Evil eye, 107-109

Faith, 24, 56, 69
Falfurrias, 9, 12, 15, 60, 61
"Fisherman and the Snake of Many Colors, The," by Wilson M. Hudson, 133-136
Flor de Agosto, 59
Flores, Tomás, 24-25
Folklore, *passim*. *See* Folktale, Motif
Folktale, charm in, 1-8
Folktale, types of, 72; type 333, 80; type 754***, 81; type 2028, 80
Foster, Mrs., 36-37
Fuente, Antonio de la, 50-51

García, Ponciano, 53-54
Garza, Señora Concha García de la, 20
Garza, Doña Ramona, 55

"Ghost Tales," 90-96
Goethe, 2
González, Don Doroteo, 18
Gorbert, Zack, 44
Grassburr, 40
Graves, Charlie, 18
Graves, Frank, 18
Gutiérrez, Doña Encarnación, 59-60

Hacienda de los Albarcones, 88, 96-99
Headache, 36
Hernández, Señorita Eduwiges, 43
Hernández, Señora Petra Rocha de, 62
Hinguanza, Monico, 49
Hinojosas, Don Antonio, 14
Hoffman, Norman, 36
Hoffman, Mrs. N. A., 16
Horse, cure of, 39, 46-47
Horsebreaker, 38-39
Hudson, William Henry, 7
Hudson, William M., v; "To Whom God Wishes to Give He Will Give," 128-132; "The Fisherman and the Snake of Many Colors," 132-136

Ibáñez, Augustina de, 54-55

Jaramillo, Don Pedrito, v, 9-70; life, 11-18; his cures, 18-68; evaluation, 68-70

Lambert, "Don Patricio," 4
Laredo, 13, 65
Lemos, Señora Eufemia P. de, 63-65
Lerma, Felipe, 42
Llorente, Alicia, 65
Llorona, La, 73-76
Longhorns, The, by J. Frank Dobie, 3-5
Los Olmos Creek, 13, 49
Los Olmos Ranch, where Don Pedrito Jaramillo lived, 9-70 passim
Lozano, José C., 49

McAllen, Texas, 17
McNeill, Pete, 55-56
Mad dog, 46
Margaret (an epileptic), 37-38
Martínez, Pablo, 27-28

Martínez, Prisciliano, 27-28
Mathis, Texas, 33, 63
Measles, 44
Mexican folktales, passim. See Dobie, Dodson, Hudson (W. M.), Pérez
Mier, Mexico, 20
Money, mysterious, 47
Motif, 72;
  A737, 115;
  A2221.2.4, 117;
  B147.1.1.4, 115;
  B576.2, 100;
  B613.1, 132;
  C771.1, 86;
  D190, 132;
  D1242.2, 116;
  D1273, 116;
  D1713, 104;
  D1812.3.3, 115;
  D1812.5.1.4, 115;
  D2064.4, 108;
  D2071, 108;
  D2140.1, 102, 103;
  E235, 95;
  E235.1, 115;
  E235.4, 78;
  E283, 99;
  E300, 93, 94;
  E402, 94, 96, 99;
  E411, 74;
  E411.0.3, 88;
  E421.1.1, 91;
  E451.3, 92;
  E520, 100;
  E535, 102;
  E545.2, 91;
  E631.0.5, 106;
  F52, 86;
  F420.6.1, 132;
  F772.1, 86;
  G303.3.1, 87, 88;
  G303.3.1.2, 86;
  G303.3.3.1, 90;
  G303.3.3.4, 90;
  G303.3.3.15, 132;
  K231.3, 103;
  K1811, 106;
  M416.2, 81;
  N511.1, 100;
  N532, 101;
  Q251, 114;
  Q502.1, 81;
  V22, 74;
  V132, 115;
  V220, 102

New York, 30

"Niño Perdido, El," 103
Nosebleed, 45
Nueces River, 12, 28, 33, 55

O'Connor, Tom, 3
Onions, as a cure, 58-59

Paisano, formerly in Starr and now in Brooks County, 11, 14
Paralytic, 30
Pérez, Soledad, v; "Mexican Folklore from Austin, Texas," 71-127
Post Office Department, 15
Prescriptions, written, 67-68
Prickly pear, 45-46, 62-63, 100
"Proverbs and Sayings," 118-125

Ramírez, Doña Mariana, 33
Ramírez, Mariano, 46-47
Ramírez, Salomé, 33, 34
Ranch: Davis, 52; Dobie, 50; La Coma, 44; Las Cabras, 11, 14, 18, 22; Las Parrillas, 18; Los Olmos, 9-70 passim; Lost, 9; San Pedro, 20, 21, 22
Rattlesnake, 21
Refugio, 62
Regalo, Colonel Toribio, 39
"Remedies," 106-114
Rheumatism, 35
"Riddles," 126-127
Rio Grande River, 12, 21, 52
Rodríguez, Dionisio, 18
Ruiz, Miguel, 51
Ruiz, Silverio, 38-39

Saenz, Marcelino, 56
Saenz, Señora María, 65
"Saints' Miracles," 102-106
San Antonio, 13, 58
Sandia, in Jim Wells County, 44
San Diego, Texas, 19, 63, 64, 65
Sayings, 118-125
Shepherd, cure of, 49, 70
Singing, of Don Pedrito, 50
Sinton, Texas, 63

Socorro, New Mexico, 41
Soldier herb, 57
Spells, 116-117
Spirit of Don Pedrito Jaramillo, 60, 63, 63-65, 65-66
Strickland, Dr. J. S., 16
Superstition, 114-118
Susto, 42, 57-58, 110-113
Sutherland, Mabel, 28-31
Sutherland, William, 28, 29, 34

"Tales of Buried Treasure," 96-102
"Tales of the Devil," 86-90
Tatema, 129
Texas Folklore Society, v, 10; Pub. X, 10; Pub. XII, 128; Pub. XXI, 128
Thompson, Stith, 72. See Folktale (types of), Motif
Tijerina, Fernando M., 65
Timon, Harry, 34-35
Tone the Bell Easy, 10
Tongues of the Monte, by J. Frank Dobie, 7-8
"To Whom God Wishes to Give He Will Give," by Wilson M. Hudson, 128-132
Townshend, R. B., The Tenderfoot in New Mexico, 2
Treviño, Don Lino, 57, 61
Treviño, wife of Tomás, 52-53

Valdéz, Simón, 45
Vela, Chat, 31-32
Virgen de Guadalupe, 66
Virgen de San Juan de los Lagos, 66
Vow, 62-63, 65

Walker, Jim, 69
Wallace, Bigfoot, 2
Water, to drink as a cure, 45
"Weeping Woman, The," 73-76
Whisky, 33, 39
World War II, 65

Yorktown, Texas, 24

Zamora, Señora Rosa, 25-27